P9-DFC-749

KEEPING CUSTOMERS FOR LIFE

KEEPING CUSTOMERS FOR LIFE

JOAN KOOB CANNIE

WITH

DONALD CAPLIN

amacom

American Management Association

Library of Congress Cataloging-in-Publication Data

Cannie, Joan Koob.
    Keeping customers for life / Joan K. Cannie, with Donald Cap-
lin.
        p.   cm.
    Includes bibliographical references and index.
    ISBN 0-8144-5008-3 (hardcover)
    1. Customer service—United States.   2. Consumer satisfac-
tion—United States.   I. Caplin, Donald.   II. Title.
HF5415.5.C36   1991   90-53213
658.8′12—dc20   CIP

Printing number

10   9   8   7   6   5   4   3   2   1

Contents

KEEPING CUSTOMERS FOR LIFE

Introduction

Keeping Customers for Life

In companies throughout the United States—advertising claims to the contrary—a sincere dedication to satisfying customers is rare.

In our recent survey of nearly 200 major U.S. corporations, 57 percent *said* that customer satisfaction was their first priority. However, 73 percent—almost three out of four—*also said* that the only way to survive is on price competition. (Our survey is in the Appendix. We invite you to complete it yourself.)

As a specific example, most U.S. automakers never thought of their work as satisfying customers by making quality cars. Until, of course, their image—and their earnings—were hammered by quality imports. Automakers are not the only culprits.

Unfortunately for the U.S. economy, most people in hotels, hospitals, brokerage offices, department stores, banks, government agencies, insurance offices—anywhere—rarely think of themselves as customer "satisfiers." They are data entry processors, sales supporters, bookkeepers, or salespeople. They are managers, lawyers, nurses, or Indian chiefs. Regardless of their titles or job descriptions, most of them view the customer either as a pest—or as "not my job."

The nasty result of this customer indifference costs the average company from 15 percent to 30 percent of gross sales. And, as we explain in Chapter 7, preventing this waste can send these lost dollars right to the bottom line.

Such prevention—and the cost savings that result—usually demands transforming an organization's culture. It calls for training people at all levels to be customer-friendly; implementing new strategies, policies, and systems; and getting managers to "think customer" and to model their commitment as Customer-Champions. But as America's leading-edge companies have shown, the payoff of these changes can be both dramatic and rapid.

Many companies have reclaimed lost markets, rebuilt damaged customer relationships, cut costs sharply, and increased market share. Nearly all are their industry's leaders. For example:

- Florida Power & Light reports it saves about $1.25 million per week from its quality improvement programs.[1]
- Before reclaiming its market with the low-maintenance quality machines its customers wanted, Xerox lost over 40 percent of its sales to the Japanese—*in an industry it invented.*
- Federal Express credits its competitive leadership to "customer dedication." It will climb a mountain in a snowstorm or charter a private jet to deliver an urgent letter.
- Companies like Disney, Marriott, Amex, and USA Today are leading the way in quality products and services. And in so doing, they have gained a nearly untouchable competitive advantage.

Few executives realize that when they differentiate themselves from their competitors with customer-driven service (CDS), their customers will gladly pay a higher premium for their product or service. Furthermore, most companies that have initiated a CDS process have found that the return on investment (ROI) is outstanding—an average of 10 to 1. In our view, this means that any American business that practices what it preaches about customer satisfaction can walk home dominating any market.

The competitive payoff doesn't apply just to big companies: Any size business can play and win. In fact, small is easier, as you'll see in our report in Chapter 8 on Price's Market, a convenience store in Richmond, Virginia, run by Bob and Candy Kocher.

However, in our experience, the best work in customer satisfaction is being done by individual managers—line and staff—within all kinds of companies. Here are some Customer-Champions you'll meet in the course of this book:

- Glen Evans at C&P Telephone, who uses training, personal commitment, and political savvy to empower future managers for the drastic changes he anticipates for his company in the 1990s
- Wanda Draper at National Aquarium in Baltimore, who combines personal leadership, training, and some kind of magic to get part-time workers at minimum wages to take wonderful care of 1.4 million visitors a year
- Wynn Tyner, whose inspired leadership and innovative reward systems have made the Camelback Inn Marriott's top hotel—and it's a *resort*. . . . (People on vacation at posh resorts are especially hard to please.)

- Barbra McKenzie at Bell Atlantic, who is building the esteem needs, confidence, and people skills of thousands of operators with a simple but powerful training program

We call these Customer-Champions "islands" of service excellence.

Some are involved in companywide programs; others are using their own mixture of leadership, commitment, and politicking to help assure their company's competitive edge. We present their stories in small vignettes throughout this book to show that any manager can take this process and use it anywhere. It's not difficult to do. You just need to put it in place and keep it going.

The numerous worksheets throughout this book show how to put theory into action. We help you analyze where you are now and plan what to do, and we show you how you can do it.

From our own experience as consultants and trainers and from the experience of client companies, we have distilled a twelve-step basic strategy to provide superb service and help ensure 100 percent customer satisfaction. When most, if not all, of these twelve steps are at work, you can be pretty certain you have an exceptional, innovative, service-quality organization. Furthermore, it will usually be an exceptional financial performer and have a strong leader at its helm.

To verify our own experiences, we recently collected data from 200 companies in order to learn what they were doing about satisfying their customers. Specifically, we asked about the leaders' vision and how that vision had translated into action: What had worked? What were the effects on the organization? What were the roles and behaviors of the managers? From the responses we distilled common elements in the successes and learned whether they were company-specific or applicable to any company, large or small, service or manufacturing.

(The findings from this research are distributed throughout the book where they illustrate a point in one of the twelve steps. Complete results are summarized and analyzed in the Appendix.)

The most successful companies—in terms of margins and market share—use these twelve steps and others to help achieve 100 percent customer satisfaction. And it's good news for America, because we are being seriously challenged now in world trade markets, and we need this expertise.

One of the U.S.'s thorniest problems today is the decline of our productivity caused by the expansion of our service industries, now over 80 percent of the economy. Currently, service productivity runs at about 60 percent of manufacturing productivity. So every worker who moves from manufacturing to service equals roughly a 40 percent decline in productivity. "Continued growth of services, with no acceleration of their productivity," writes Gabriel Paul, former head of IBM's Quality Programs, "is a sure prescription for America's decline as a competitive, high-wage technological and industry power."

For Those Who Create Customers' Problems

This book is for everyone from chief executive to frontline supervisor. That's quite a range, we know. But almost everyone in an organization does have an impact on customers, whether or not you see customers or are so far removed from them you've forgotten who customers are.

We direct this book to those managers who have the greatest impact and who are responsible for over 80 percent of customer problems:

• *Senior managers and owners.* You pretty much determine the culture of your organization, because you are the ones who have established the strategies, policies, and systems that drive your organization. So if your customers are not well-served, you, and you alone, must lead the change. It will take new customer commitment and leadership behaviors, which you can learn from this book.

• *Middle managers.* Even though you may rarely see customers, you create most of the problems customers encounter, primarily through the decisions you make or don't make. Furthermore, you model behavior for a cadre of *internal customers* up and down the line, all of whom ultimately have an impact on the way external customers are served. So, while most companies spend big training dollars on frontline people, you need training most. This book will give you the skills you need to help your company provide 100 percent customer satisfaction. Incidentally, you also stand to gain the greatest payback. "Keeping customers" really is the new fast track in growing organizations—not a bad skill to know in these days of restructuring and massive layoffs of middle managers.

• *Frontline supervisors (on the way up).* The restructuring just mentioned is the route more and more companies are taking to get rid of too many management levels and get closer to their customers. This presents a seldom seen window of opportunity for the men and women who do interact with customers to move up quickly. But you have to know the rules of the game and how to keep score. This book teaches you both.

A special note to entrepreneurs: Over 600,000 new companies are started each year, and nearly 90 percent of them fail. There are of course many reasons for this terrible failure rate, but most research points to poor management as the major factor.[2] So keep your eye on your customers. You can get so caught up in such concerns as accounting and legal fine points, raising money, and finding office space that you can easily lose sight of the single most important ingredient in the success of your venture: the customer.

Keeping Customers for Life

Keeping customers for life through 100 percent satisfaction can happen only through people relationships. You can be fairly certain that your customers will be poorly served—

- If your people are unmotivated, disgruntled, or having a bad day;
- If they are not trained or empowered to solve customers' problems or provide quality service;
- If the boss treats them badly or otherwise devalues them;
- If you and other managers model "the customer is a pest"; or
- If you make decisions and establish systems without considering the impact on your customers.

So while it's good news that we have the technology to solve our international competition problems, it's *better* news that the solutions come from treating people—customers and employees—really well: listening, responding to needs, transforming managers from taskmasters to Customer-Champions and coaches. In return you get ordinary people stretching past their own ideas of what they can do—a turned-on work force producing quality and churning out superb service. And everybody—managers, stockholders, customers, and employees alike—winning, while you drive costs down and earnings up.

This book tells you how to take wonderful care of your customers and the people who take care of them. Make this your number one strategic priority. Then take on any competitors and beat them fairly, openly, and hands down.

Notes

1. "Florida Power & Light Company," American Productivity Center, Case Study 39, Houston, Tex.: 1984.
2. U.S. President's Study on Small Business, 1983.

Part I

The Importance of Service in Today's Business World

One

Service in Today's Economy

Almost overnight our economy has changed. Just as we once changed from an agricultural society into an industrial society, the United States has now changed into what John Naisbitt has labeled an information society. ("Farmer. Laborer. Clerk." is how Naisbitt describes the history of work in the United States.[1]) Whatever we call it, we have entered a period dominated by companies that *perform* rather than *produce*. As a result, customers in this new era focus on service quality far more than any other factor—so much so that making customers happy through service quality has become the new fast track of the American economy.

Yet few of our organizations are customer-friendly or service-driven. In fact, most big companies have lost control of their service quality and, with it, the competitive advantage that service excellence provides. And this at a time when over 80 percent of the American work force is engaged in service activities.[2]

If this last statement seems hard to believe, think about how many different organizations exist only to perform services:

Banking	Entertainment
Investments	Travel
Hospitals	Real estate
Health care	Law
Insurance	Data processing
Education	Communications
Training	Public utilities
Publishing	Religion
Transportation	Charity
Equipment leasing	The armed forces
Credit cards	All government: local,
Express delivery	state, and federal

If you have any doubt about the scope of service in our economy, open your checkbook and see where you are spending your money.

9

Even from those companies that do produce products, customers expect service quality as part of every purchase. So we have an overwhelming majority of our economic machine *selling service* but only a *tiny minority* of companies really delivering it. What an opportunity for a competitive advantage that costs you virtually nothing! Because the hard reality is that more and more customers are deciding to do business with those organizations that really do satisfy their requirements—not just talk about it. And they are walking away from those that don't.

With the overwhelming advantage service quality provides, why are so few companies committed to it? Probably because:

1. The demand for quality care is fairly new, and most companies have been getting away without providing it.

2. Top management is just now realizing that customer-driven service is a *strategic process*. Advertisements, slogans, and lip service won't do it. It takes top-level commitment, new management decisions, changed attitudes, strategies and systems, customer-friendly behaviors, and a lot more. This is a big job in any company, and it can't happen overnight.

3. Finally, and probably most importantly, the managers in most U.S. companies have not yet accepted the responsibility for satisfying customers, even though fully 80 percent of their problems stem from management policies, systems, and decisions. If managers do anything at all, typically they train frontline personnel. And there's nothing wrong in that. But the front line can't correct the problems of rigid systems, frustrating rules, and cost-driven policies that are the sources of most customers' problems. These are fixable only by managers. And most managers are so far removed from customers that they've forgotten who customers are.

Therein lies the real secret of Japan's success. Yes, most of us are weary of "The Japanese Miracle" story and how they are outstripping the United States in world markets. But the Japanese are doing *something* that's enabling them to hammer American companies in the productivity head, not only in automobiles, but in consumer electronics, office automation, and—now on their "hot list"—real estate, banks, motion pictures, and construction.

One study indicates that the Japanese are so successful *not* because their culture emphasizes productivity (their absenteeism, turnover, and speed are worse than ours). Rather, their "secret" is, quite simply, management strategy: a commitment to customers for life.[3]

Chapter 2 examines some current business strategies to see what the Japanese do that we mostly don't do.

Notes

1. John Naisbitt, *Megatrends* (New York: Warner Books, 1984), p. 5.
2. U.S. Bureau of Labor Statistics.
3. Andrew Weiss, "Simple Truths of Japanese Manufacturing," *Harvard Business Review*, July 1984.

Two

The Real Japanese Miracle: Customer-Driven Service Quality

There are at least five different base strategies used in business today:

1. *Commodity Strategy.* This strategy assumes that your product or service is essentially the same as others in the market. You attempt to differentiate on price and/or volume. Internally, the strategy requires ruthless cost-cutting, focus on productivity in both blue- and white-collar areas, little investment in improving the business, and large volume to make up for slim margins. The Japanese adopted this strategy before and after World War II and abandoned it as worthless in the late 1950s.

2. *Technology-Driven Strategy.* This involves focusing solely on building temporary monopolies by staying technologically ahead of your competitors. It usually requires massive investments in R&D; high-powered specialists, such as engineers, who are driven to achieve excellence in their field (whether or not this "excellence" is relevant to customer needs); shortened production cycles, multiple changes in products already in production; and large investments in fixing problems out in the field.

This strategy is uniquely American. Despite their reputation, the Japanese have never seriously considered this strategy. Instead, they have let U.S. companies do the innovation, then pirated it and improved it.

3. *Quality-Driven Strategy.* This strategy is currently in vogue in the United States, although it passed its peak of popularity in Japan in the early 1970s. Begun by the work of two American engineers in postwar Japan, quality improvement is now routine at nearly all levels of every Japanese company. However, it is no longer seen as the only requirement for business success.

Currently in the United States, millions of dollars are being spent on quality. A huge industry has developed in the belief that improved quality will make customers buy. But with few exceptions, practitioners (e.g., General Motors and USX) of Total Quality Improvement (TQI) are still losing markets to the Japanese. So what is wrong? The answer is: *Quality doesn't go far enough.* It doesn't deal with *what customers want* or with the *service relationship that customers are demanding.*

Ask any TQI guru, "What is quality?" and the answer is, "Defect-free conformance to customer requirements." But, too often, in TQI the last person involved in the process is the customer. So, while no one will argue with improving quality, it usually means meeting *engineering* requirements.

J. M. Juran (who practically invented TQI) points out that Americans typically respond to Japanese competition by:

- Lobbying for import restrictions
- Starting quality circles
- Setting quality incentives
- Measuring the cost of quality

What's missing is a grand strategy putting the customer into the picture—from the business plan to the delivery of your product and/or service.

4. *Service-Driven Strategy.* According to this strategy, neither price, technology, nor quality is sufficient to differentiate your product or service from your competition. They only allow you to stay competitive. Therefore, to attract customers, you add "extra value" by how you deliver service. The "unconditional service guarantee" is an example, as is Federal Express's "absolutely, positively . . . overnight."

The focus on service makes it difficult, but not impossible, to ignore the customer. Still companies can fail at this strategy by delivering on time and happily accepting complaints and returns for products that no one wants.

Some of our most successful companies use this service-driven strategy: Nordstrom, American Express, L. L. Bean, Caterpillar (parts anywhere in the world within forty-eight hours), McDonald's. But there are failures: J. Bildner's, airlines with all first-class seats, possibly Sears (the jury is still out). But if companies simply go all out to provide extra services without building in customer input, the costs can ruin them.

5. *Customer-Driven Strategy.* Closely related to service-driven strategy, customer-driven strategy is truly the key to the Japanese "miracle." The current English translation of this strategy is "Quality Function Development," which makes it seem devilishly complex and hopelessly mired in engineering jargon. But the message is actually deceptively simple: *Bring the customer's voice in-house* so you can build your policies and your

products around your customer's needs. Japan's leading manufacturing and service companies use this strategy, while American executives struggle to copy control charts and fishbone diagrams to master the quality-driven strategy that Japan has long since outgrown.

Customer-driven strategy requires quality *and* service excellence at every level. In the process, customers are brought into every department of the company, and their voices heard and acted on. The long-term result of this approach is keeping customers for life.

Listening to the Customer Pays Off

Interesting question: How many customers have you talked to in the past year? In the past five years?

Interesting fact: A recent MIT study showed that 80 percent of technological innovations come from customers.

Interesting case history: Vanport is a lumber company in the American Northwest. American companies have never sold much lumber to Japan, and Vanport was determined to find out why. First they spent years traveling in Japan, finding out what wood Japanese like. Then they invited some Japanese executives from lumber-buying companies over here to talk to their foremen on how Japanese grade lumber and how they are particular about the color and cut of the wood.

After two years, Vanport felt confident enough to show its product to Japanese executives. It even went so far as to build a Japanese guest house here for overseas visitors. The Japanese were impressed with Vanport's sensitivity to their needs (the guest house was the only comfortable place some had found in the States).

Vanport now exports 90 percent of its product to Japan.[1]

Interesting statistics: A study by the Strategic Planning Institute of Cambridge, Massachusetts, has looked at the difference between companies that customers rate above-average and below-average in service.

Those in the top half of service ratings grow twice as fast, charge about 10 percent more, and return 1,100 percent more on sales![2]

In a study completed a few years ago, the U.S. Office of Consumer Affairs found that proactive customer care can turn into a significant profit center.* Industries as diverse as banking, utilities, consumer durable goods, retail, and automotive service are actually earning up to 400 percent return on investment by seeking and handling complaints.[3] (See Figure 2-1.)

---

* That is, profits attributable to complaint handling divided by the cost of handling complaints.

Figure 2-1. ROI by corporate complaint-handling units.

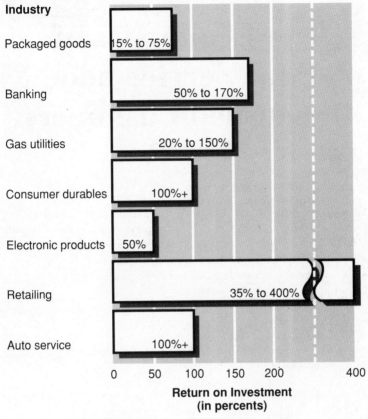

Reprinted by courtesy of Learning Dynamics, Inc.

Notes

1. Tom Peters, *Thriving on Chaos* (New York: Knopf, 1988), p. 84.
2. Robert D. Buzzell and Bradley T. Gale, *The PIMS Principles* (New York: Free Press, 1987), Ch. 6.
3. TARP (Technical Assistance Research Programs Institute), "Consumer Complaint Handling in America: An Update Study," (Washington, D.C.: U.S. Office of Consumer Affairs, 1986).

Three

The Economics of Poor Service and Dissatisfied Customers

The Consumer Affairs study discussed in Chapter 2 reveals that 96 percent of your unhappy customers don't complain to you—but they do tell at least ten other people about their problem. Those few who do complain will remain customers *if* their problem is resolved.[1]

So what does this cost your organization? Here's an interesting exercise on what an "average" customer is worth.

Profit = long-term profit from a customer
+ word of mouth to 10 friends
+ money saved from avoiding the cost of doing it over (response cost)
− cost of handling a complaint.

What does it cost to lose customers—the 96 percent who don't complain to you but who do tell others about you?

Cost = what an average customer is worth
× how many customers you lose per year (for the average company it's 25 percent of the customer base)
+ the cost of the lost potential business from an average of 10 friends of each lost customer.

For example, an average supermarket customer is worth $22,000 over five years. A medium-size market has approximately 1,000 customers. If it loses 25 percent per year and each tells at least ten friends, total it up and you're talking about millions of dollars in lost or potential business.

Worksheet 1 has an exercise to help you determine how much poor service costs your organization.

Worksheet 1. The Cost of Poor Service

To estimate how much poor service costs your organization, calculate the following:

Lost Revenue	*Your Cost*
1. What your average customer spends in a year	_____
2. Number of customers lost each year (for average company, 25 percent)	_____
3. Revenue lost from lost customers (#1 × #2)	_____
4. Lost revenue from people ex-customers talk to (#3 × 10)	_____

Labor Costs	*Your Cost*
5. Time redoing things not done right the first time	_____
6. Time spent on warranty repairs	_____
7. Time spent apologizing to customers	_____
8. Time spent responding to government agencies, consumer complaint bureaus, etc.	_____

Other Costs	*Your Cost*
9. Cost of shipping express instead of regular	_____
10. Cost of collections from angry customers who refuse to pay	_____
11. Cost of liability insurance	_____
12. Legal costs	_____
13. Telephone costs for apologizing, explaining, etc.	_____
14. Postage costs for reshipping, apologizing, explaining, etc.	_____
Total (add numbers 3 through 14)	=======

Reprinted by courtesy of Learning Dynamics, Inc.

Why Companies Don't Improve Service

There are powerful economic advantages for an organization that provides quality service, and there are heavy costs in lost market share for not doing so. What, then, is the mystery? Why *don't* companies routinely make 100 percent customer satisfaction their number one priority?

It's not that companies haven't tried to fix the problem. They have. In fact, top management has spent millions of dollars on market research, consultants of every kind, training of every description, and, most recently, on total quality improvement (in hope of copying the Japanese).

All of these strategies do help—that is, quality improvement usually does improve quality; training does train people in new skills; research does provide information on which to base decisions; consultants do provide careful studies and detailed reports on the problem. But none, by themselves, guarantee 100 percent customer satisfaction.

Training has helped so many companies solve so many problems that it's difficult to explain why training frontline customer service personnel doesn't permanently improve the quality of service. It does help frontline staff cope. And it does provide selective solutions. But even the best trained, most dedicated, and highly skilled customer service people cannot single-handedly overcome unfriendly policies, solve problems they are not empowered to solve, break company rules in favor of customers, or change a corporate culture that thinks of customers as pests.

So while training may well provide the skills that frontline people need, without top management priority on customers, much training is wasted. Even worse, people who receive customer service training are often demotivated. They learn how to do it right and how to put customers first, but company policies and managers won't allow it. No wonder so many customer service representatives suffer undue stress, become surly with customers, and eventually quit.

Most market research is aimed at prospects—not customers—to determine the market acceptance of new products or services. Furthermore, research of any kind is seldom used by managers to make customer-focused decisions, let alone incorporated into product and service development, production, and marketing (another secret of the Japanese "miracle").

Finally, if customers do say what they want—and it disagrees with management's view of things—their responses are generally ignored: "What do customers know?"

Consultants in untold numbers have been summoned to study the problem. Today, so many reports have been written and so many dollars spent—without result—that most companies now have a ceiling on how much even top executives can spend on these services. If executives read and acted on the information and advice contained in these reports, they'd probably get results. But, like research studies, these reports are usually not distributed to decision makers and are not mandated for action.

Quality improvement programs have helped company after company and in some cases saved huge amounts of wasted costs. However, this improvement has occurred largely in product quality (and in a few service systems such as checkout lines, crowd control, fast food distribution, and sometimes even on-time departures). But improving the quality of products takes a completely different process (internal focus) from improving the quality of service (external, customer focus).

So, while companies have spent vast amounts of money to improve service quality, they have not gotten what they hoped they were buying: happy customers. How can you crack this nut? There is no one answer, but a combination of activities embodied in an ongoing process that is focused on customers.

To better understand the interaction between an organization and its customers, let's examine the Dynamic System Theory.

The Dynamic System Theory

The Dynamic System Theory is the work of the eminent scientist Ludwig von Bertalanffy (biologist, philosopher, and founder of the General System Theory).[2] It has revolutionized the field of human behavior because it represents a new way of looking at people and our environment. It says that we humans are not just passive victims of our environment and conditioning. Rather we have the ability to create and control our world. This control—and its corresponding responsibility—also applies to organizations. Here is how it works.

The system is composed of three parts: input, feedback, and reality, as shown in Figure 3-1.

Here's how it operates in an organization. First you have the input into the system; in this case:

Negative Input

- No customer focus or commitment (lip service and advertising slogans don't count)
- Customer requirements unknown
- No performance measurement standards or goals
- Strategies and systems that serve the organization—not customers
- Employees not trained or empowered to care for customers
- No attempt to solve problems or improve

Such input produces an almost guaranteed:

Feedback Of

- Poor public image and bad press
- Customers angry and telling others
- Pressure on productivity, profits, and earnings
- High costs of waste, mistakes, rework
- High turnover and low morale in frontline personnel
- Lost market share and competitive edge

Finally, there is *reality,* which comes in two parts.

First, reality is the way you and other people in your organization see things. In this negative case, customer satisfaction is an afterthought

Figure 3-1. Dynamic System: negative.

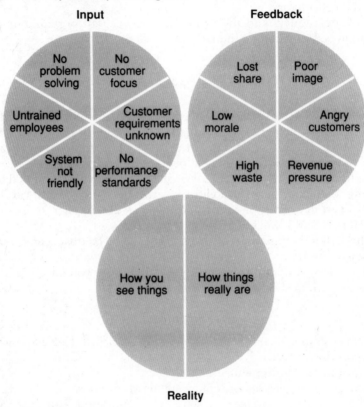

Reprinted by courtesy of Learning Dynamics, Inc.

at best. This view determines your organizational culture (input) and guarantees built-in customer dissatisfaction.

Second, reality is what really *is*, whether you see it that way or not. And the reality is: *Customers really do call the tune. If you treat them badly or indifferently, they have many other places to go.*

Now let's look at this another way with:

Positive Input

Here the inputs are (see Figure 3-2):

- Management committed and focused on customers
- Customers' requirements known and met

Figure 3-2. Dynamic System: positive.

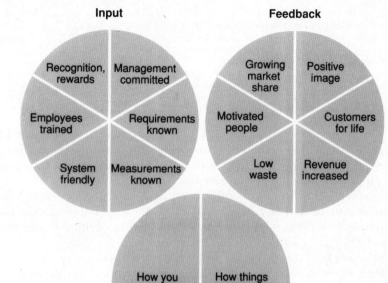

Reprinted by courtesy of Learning Dynamics, Inc.

- Performance measurements known and published
- Customer-friendly systems and strategies
- All members of the organization, including managers, trained and empowered to care for customers
- Continuous improvement recognized and rewarded

Let's see what feedback this positive input produces:

Feedback Of

- A positive company image
- Keeping customers for life
- Increased revenue and earnings

- Costs of waste slashed
- Motivated, empowered personnel
- Growing repeat business and market share

And, for the two-part reality, we have:

1. The organization's commitment to serving its customers
2. Success and growth in today's service economy

The single most important aspect of this dynamic system is that any change in the system changes the *entire system*. For example, if you change your view of reality, you change both your input and feedback. Change your input and you change your feedback.

This is another way of saying that you, and your organization's other executives, are in control and are responsible for what happens to it. This includes its treatment of customers, its competitive position in the market, its image and earnings, its success or failure.

Now let's take this theory of reality a step further.

Most executives today—even though they run service operations—are managing by outdated models (input). They are using the techniques developed by and for industrial corporations, which once represented the majority of America's business.

Figure 3-3 illustrates the difference between service- and product-driven management.

There are striking input differences between managing a service operation and managing a manufacturing operation. The realities of customer-driven service shown in Figure 3-4 present a model for managing to achieve service quality. It relates the key elements of customer-driven service to both the conventional industrial model of management and the newer service model of management.

Reality 1: Priority

The industrial model defines service as either a nice-to-have or a necessary evil. But customer-driven service takes a top-down, whole-organization approach that almost always involves a change in corporate culture.

High-quality service is such a powerful, competitive weapon that it is regarded by Federal Express, Nordstrom, Disney, and other leading-edge companies as an essential part of business strategy—not as a "nice-to-have" or "necessary evil" feature.

Federal Express, whose entire business is based on priority of service, will do whatever it takes to keep its customers number 1. When deliveries can't be made via the usual channels (for example, medical

Figure 3-3. Service-driven vs. product-driven management styles.

Service-Driven	Product-Driven
Package of benefits delivered via a relationship (e.g., telephone service).	Tangible commodity (e.g., telephones).
Open to customer (e.g., automobile showroom).	Closed to customers (e.g., automobile factory).
Labor-intensive; concern for employee motivation and attitudes critical. Employee is sole contact with customer. If disgruntled, employee can do irreparable harm.	Employee (labor) may sabotage product, but final inspection can correct.
Output is intangible and difficult to measure (customers must rely on reputation of the service firm or government regulation).	Products are things; customers can see, feel, and test before purchase. Many products are also covered by money-back guarantee.
Customers are participants in the process (e.g., fast food). Use this participation to control demand.	Inventory used to control demand.
Production and consumption occur simultaneously—cannot be stored (e.g., express delivery).	Inventory can be stored.
Perishable; if not used, sale may be lost forever (e.g., empty airline seat, cancelled dental appointment).	Inventory can be stored.
Demand is variable and cyclical (e.g., noon lunch hour, Thanksgiving weekend flights).	Demand tied more to economic savings.
Site location (e.g., hotels, retail stores, banks) dictated by customer.	Site location dictated by organizational needs (e.g., labor pool, transportation).

Reprinted by courtesy of Learning Dynamics, Inc.

supplies needed for an operation), Federal Express actually charters Lear jets to make deliveries. This happens several times a year; FedEx loses money on these particular deals, but it keeps its pledge of overnight delivery.[3]

Schlitz (beer), however, is a sorry story of putting cost-cutting ahead of customer preferences. By switching to lower-cost syrup and hop pellets and cutting the brewing cycle by 50 percent, it did indeed have a higher short-term return. But within a few years, the company's market position fell from number two to number seven, and the stock price collapsed from $69 per share to $5.[4]

It is no exaggeration to say that organizations that cannot, or do not,

Figure 3-4.   Realities of customer-driven service.

Factor	Conventional Wisdom (Industrial Model)	Reality of Today's Service Economy
Priority of service	Nice-to-have or necessary evil	A top management concern
Method of service	Corrective action	Customer-driven service management
Customer requirements	Unknown or assumed	Researched and pulsed on a regular basis. Used as basis for decisions
Strategies and systems	Serve organizational and/or internal quality needs	Serve customer needs by doing right things right
Management style	Organizational focus; costs and productivity top priority	Customer-driven; focused on learning and meeting customers' requirements
Responsibility for customer-driven service	Entry-level help trained in tasks, not in service quality delivery	Everyone empowered and trained to serve customers—either external or internal.
Motivation and recognition	Rewards are occasional, unplanned, informal	Rewards, recognition, and celebrations: regular, planned, and public
Performance measurement	Service quality can't be measured	Customer-centered goals and measures, written and publicly displayed
Communications and feedback	Top down	Interactive

Reprinted by courtesy of Learning Dynamics, Inc.

put their customers first will be left further and further behind. The competitive market leaders know this and make service quality a top management priority.

Reality 2: Method

In the industrial model, service is reactive—"Send them to the complaint department."

Under the service model, service quality is proactive. It demands a clear, up-to-date understanding of customers' requirements, a goal-centered service strategy, managers who are committed and trained to "think customer," and customer-friendly systems for delivering service. In addition, since customer relations mirror employee relations, it demands carefully selected, motivated, and well-trained people. Service is first and foremost a relationship, not between the customer and the organization, but between the customer and your employee. So if you hope to take wonderful care of customers, first you need to take wonderful care of the caretakers.

Reality 3: Customer Requirements

Almost every description of quality improvement uses the phrase "meeting customer requirements." Yet very few managers (or even executives) know what customer requirements really are, let alone how to meet them. What they really do is meet engineers' standards—a process called "conformance to requirements."

To provide genuine service quality, you need to ask customers what they require, what they expect, and what they consider good service. Furthermore, you need to keep asking them every few months; customers are moving targets. Then you need to distribute what you learn to your managers and mandate its use in every decision-making nook and cranny of your group.

Reality 4: Strategies and Systems

Using the industrial model, today's managers set standards that serve organizational and system needs. Serving customers is usually an afterthought. Managers seldom see service quality as a major strategic thrust and almost never as a powerful competitive weapon. (This latter is particularly true for industries that need to differentiate themselves from the pack.) Not that companies have deliberately made their service systems pitifully poor; they have simply been neglected and allowed to evolve on their own.

Jan Carlzon turned the Scandinavian Airlines System from an $8 million loss to a $71 million profit in two years by dedicating the company to a service quality philosophy.[5] He infused all twenty thousand SAS employees with an obsessive commitment to customer service. As just one example of this across-the-board dedication, the company decided to train frontline employees to take responsibility for doing whatever they could to keep customers happy. When passengers at one airport were delayed by equipment failure and feeling somewhat grumpy, the gate attendant decided she would get them free coffee and donuts. The airline's own kitchen, clearly not yet focused on the new policy, claimed it was unauthorized. The attendant then went to a competitor and bought the coffee and donuts herself. She was reimbursed and commended.

Reality 5: Management Style

Typically, the executives who create the systems—and who make the decisions about rules, policies and procedures—never see customers. So it's no surprise that they don't think about them when they make decisions. As a result, most managers are focused on the needs and convenience of the organization, not the customers. The examples everyone relates to are airlines that overbook; hospitals that demand information before providing treatment; banks that give you a hard time when you try to get your money; and motor vehicle departments that are so inefficient they require three-hour waits.)

In the companies that are known for exemplary service, all managers focus on customers and "doing the right things right" to assure 100 percent customer satisfaction.

To achieve customer-driven service means that first, you need to learn what customers want by asking them, and, from this information, establish customer-based measures of service quality and satisfaction. Second, after your measurements are defined, you need to communicate them to your organization through goals. Third, you need to invest in *training*—especially training all managers to evaluate the impact of their decisions on customers. Fourth, establish rewards. For example, use your satisfaction measures in performance evaluations as a basis for promotions and raises. Finally, don't lose sight of the fact that this is an on-going process. Constantly monitor and constantly improve—with everyone in the organization participating in the process. And celebrate a lot.

Reality 6: Performance Measurement

Managers often argue that:

1. Service does not lend itself to standardization and therefore to control.
2. Service quality is difficult, if not impossible, to measure objectively.

There are two ways in which service quality can be measured.

The first is to gain direct information from your customers about what is important to them. For example, a restaurant may believe that an innovative menu is most important. But the customers may be primarily concerned with the ambience or speed or location. The answers to what's important to customers can come only from them. These results can then be fed back to frontline employees and agreement reached on what to measure. These measurements need to be displayed for all to see.

For example, AT&T uses a system that queries customers about the quality of service they receive and uses the responses as a basis for rewarding employees. Periodic surveys ask customers to rate such things as the quality of transmission (static, clarity, crossed lines, calls that don't go through), as well as employee performance (speed of response to questions, knowledgeability, courtesy). Technical employees are rated by customers' answers to the first type of questions; managers and customer service employees by the second. The higher the rating, the bigger the employee's bonus.

Another method for measuring service, when measurements are vague, is to calculate the cost of doing things wrong: rework, revisions, downtime, unplanned additional service calls, lost customers. Reducing these costs increases profits.

In company after company, we find that 15 to 30 percent of gross sales are wasted on poor service quality. This waste is also largely preventable and these dollars could far better be sent to the bottom line.

Reality 7: Responsibility for Customer Satisfaction

It takes the work of everyone in the organization to achieve 100 percent customer satisfaction. More people than ever before serve external customers, and all of us who never see the ultimate buyers serve internal customers. So in reality, we are all customer-service representatives.

As progressive managers have come to understand this reality, they are moving ahead with the process of Empowerment: the "E" word you'll hear more and more in the 1990s.

It means giving people at all levels the authority and responsibility to solve problems and provide service excellence. Naturally, this entails a process of training, measuring, and personal accountability. But this process potentially can provide the link between satisfied customers, motivated employees, and increased company profits. Not a bad payoff.

Reality 8: Motivation and Recognition

Managers often assume that employees will achieve the goals set for them because "that's their job." They don't reward subordinates for good performance, even with a "Thank you" or "Good job," which cost nothing.

Conversely, managers often judge failure harshly. They find a scapegoat to pinpoint blame, rather than seek ways to prevent and improve through problem solving. All this creates a devaluing corporate culture that ultimately gets passed on to customers.

Never forget that service is a relationship between your employees and your customers. If you are devaluing your employees, that is the message they will pass on to customers. To help guarantee service excellence, take good care of your caretakers: Build their self esteem, value them, pay attention to their day-to-day successes. Acknowledge, reward, and celebrate both effort and goal achievement.

Reality 9: Communications and Feedback

Finally, we have conventional wisdom saying all communication and feedback must come from the top down. If executives speak clearly and subordinates listen well, the industrial model pronounces communication a success.

What we really need today is two-way communication. Yes, top management keeps the troops informed about what is going on. But frontline people also let executives know what's on their mind—and the customer's mind. The process known as Total Employee Involvement (TEI) appears to provide the solution to the "information, participation, service excellence" problem.

Notes

1. TARP (Technical Assistance Research Programs Institute), "Consumer Complaint Handling in America: An Update Study," (Washington, D.C.: U.S. Office of Consumer Affairs, 1986).
2. Ludwig von Bertalanffy, *General System Theory* (New York: George Braziller, 1968), Ch. 5.
3. Tom Peters, *Thriving on Chaos* (New York: Knopf, 1988), p. 292.
4. Robert D. Bruzzell and Bradley T. Gale, *The PIMS Principles* (New York: Free Press, 1987) p. 116.
5. Jan Carlzon, *Moments of Truth* (New York: Ballinger, 1987).

Four

Barriers to Service Excellence

In the preceding chapters, we've examined some of the powerful reasons for serving our customers well. Since the case is so strongly in favor of being customer-friendly and service-driven, let's examine why most companies are not and the barriers they face in providing customer-driven service.*

Twelve Barriers to Customer-Driven Service

Let us examine twelve difficulties a company may face while trying to provide the best service to its customers.

1. *Company policies that exist for company convenience and control.* Such policies inhibit everyone's ability to satisfy customers. Example: A patient comes to a hospital emergency room in need of care. He or she must provide the insurance information before any treatment.

2. *Job specialization.* Seldom can one person provide the full spectrum of services to customers. For example, a mortgage application: A clerk takes the application, someone else processes it, someone else does a credit check, someone else sets up the account, etc. Meanwhile, the customer squirms.

3. *No coordination of the service process.* For example, the sales, production, shipping, accounting, and credit people function in an uncoordinated fashion, producing delays and miscommunication.

4. *Decision-making power that is too remote from customers.* For example, a checkout clerk at a supermarket can accept a customer's check for

---

* We gratefully acknowledge the contribution of Sean McAlea of Learning Dynamics to this section.

$98.75, but not one for $100.83. This needs the assistant manager's approval, causing an annoying delay for your best customers who spend the most! Furthermore, this decision about check limits was made by a manager who sees customers rarely and who probably has no idea of how much this policy annoys customers.

5. *Arbitrary service policies.* For example, some stores allow you to return a shirt within fourteen days of the purchase, but not fifteen! While there can be a limit, some flexibility is necessary. A customer is reasonably entitled to be satisfied.

6. *Top priority on cost containment.* Spending extra time with an unhappy customer or giving a refund after fifteen days costs a bit more and is viewed as a loss. In reality, the only decision is: Will the customer leave feeling good or feeling bad?

7. *Indifferent, unmotivated, powerless employees.* There is little training, empowerment, or motivation for delivering service quality excellence. If employee efforts to make customers happy are not rewarded—or if employees are not empowered—they often lack motivation to solve problems. Often their own esteem needs are not met, so they *really don't care* about customers or the organization.

8. *Not enough creative problem solving.* For example, managers often see a financial accommodation as the only thing a customer wants. They see cutting a price or refunding money as evening the score, when in fact the customer has been inconvenienced and frustrated.

9. *Failure to listen to customers.* Executives don't really know what customers want and expect, so they think (hope) that just being nice will be enough. Actually, today's demanding customers want more than courtesy. But you can't guess at what they want. And only your customers know.

10. *"Customer service" is only a new name for "Complaint Department."* Customer service in many companies becomes a way to fix problems, rather than prevent them from occurring in the first place. Customers don't want problems at any time and are not served well by firefighting.

11. *Frontline contact people are powerless to solve most customers' problems.* Since 80 percent of the problems are management-related, they take the heat and are supposed to smile. But the poor decisions that created the problems, and the authority to fix them, are all in the domain of managers (who are focused on costs and who see customers as pests).

12. *Company dishonesty.* No other way to put it—some companies lie or promise more than they can deliver. Some examples: A mail order house that advertises an item for sale knowing full well that if they don't get *x* number of orders for it, they won't bother placing the production order. Or an airline that tells passengers the flight will depart thirty minutes late, and thirty minutes later says the equipment hasn't arrived yet.

Worksheet 2. Rate Your Organization

The following statements describe many organizations. Circle how true each statement is of your organization; rate on a scale of:

1 = Very true
2 = Somewhat true
3 = Not applicable
4 = Somewhat untrue
5 = Very untrue

_____	1. Policies established for the organization's convenience
_____	2. Overspecialization
_____	3. No coordination of the service process
_____	4. Remote policy- and decision-making
_____	5. Arbitrary service policies
_____	6. More interest in cutting costs than in loyal customers
_____	7. Indifferent, unmotivated contact personnel
_____	8. Scant creative problem-solving ability
_____	9. Managers don't really know what customers want
_____	10. Focusing on fixing—not preventing—problems
_____	11. Contact people powerless to take exceptional care of customers
_____	12. Company dishonesty—promising more than you can or will deliver
_____	Total

Score	Interpretation
12–21	Your organization does not seem to be concerned with customers.
22–31	Your organization seems to regard customers as an afterthought.
32–41	Your organization seems about average in thinking about customers.
42–51	Your organization seems concerned with customers but could improve its system for dealing with them.
52–60	Your organization seems very customer-friendly.

Reprinted by courtesy of Learning Dynamics, Inc.

Telling lies isn't confined to large corporations. Small companies lie as well, because who's to know?

Assessing Your Organization

How many of these barriers need to be overcome in your organization? The quiz in Worksheet 2 will help you rate your strengths and weaknesses.

Worksheet 3. Three Challenges

Identify what gets in the way of your organization delivering service excellence and plan to overcome these problems.

1. Which of the barriers in Worksheet 2 can you reduce, change, or eliminate?

   a. _____

   _____

   b. _____

   _____

   c. _____

   _____

2. How do you propose to correct, change, or eliminate these barriers?

   a. _____

   _____

   b. _____

   _____

   c. _____

   _____

Reprinted by courtesy of Learning Dynamics, Inc.

Which of the barriers are presently challenges for you? In Worksheet 3, write specific recommendations or ways to overcome three barriers and present your ideas at your next meeting.

Now decide how you would instruct your people to handle a few sticky customer service problems. Pretend Worksheet 4 represents your in-basket. Read the eight customer service problems your staff has reported to you. Then fill in your recommendation. Later, in the discussion of strategy in Chapter 10, we'll come back to this exercise to see what you might do differently at that point.

After you read the next five chapters, our recommended solutions to these problems will make more sense to you. However, if you want to read our answers now, they're in Chapter 10. It *is* your book.

(text continues on page 38)

Worksheet 4. In-Basket Reports to the Boss
(Re: Difficult Situations With Customers)

Directions: Your company makes stamps and labels. Your employees have reported the following problems. How will you solve them?

I. Rose, Order Desk Clerk

Situation: Customers do not mind the fact that we need to re-size their artwork to fit our specifications, but the $10 charge usually causes some disgruntled discussion.

Company's present position: Our catalog reads as follows:

> MARGINS: Camera ready copy must leave at least ⅛″ border on all four sides.
>
> REDUCE OR ENLARGE: Logos, artwork, camera-ready art, etc., add $10 net.
>
> LOGOS, ARTWORK, CAMERA-READY COPY: *No charge* when supplied by you in correct size. The quality of labels printed from your artwork will be no better than the quality of the artwork you provide. NOTE: We do not supply logos, special artwork, or hand-drawn illustrations. Camera-ready copy must leave at least ⅛″ border on all four sides.

We plainly state our requirements for artwork and extra cost if a size change is needed. This charge is standard in the industry, and ours is at a competitive price (though it doesn't cost us any extra to change sizes).

Your Solution

_____

_____

_____

_____

_____

II. Tom, Customer Service

Situation: After I offered all the solutions available to a customer, he threatened to take his business elsewhere. Then he just hung on the phone without saying anything else . . . just silence. What should I say? It doesn't happen that often, but I'm *very* uncomfortable when it does.

(*continues*)

Worksheet 4 (*continued*)

Company's present position: We say "we are very customer service-oriented." When a problem occurs that is the fault of the company, we do everything possible to set it straight. Sometimes correcting the problem is not good enough (I think they want blood!). And sometimes we can't correct the problem, such as when we told them we could produce something we could not.

In these types of situations, management says, "Unreasonable customers are not worth having." When customers threaten to take their business elsewhere, we are told to say that we understand they have the right to do that, and we are sorry that we couldn't satisfy them.

Your Solution

_____

_____

_____

_____

_____

III. Bob, Customer Service

Situation: Customer does not understand photocopy quality until he receives his first order. He is comparing this to offset printing and demanding unrealistic quality from us. He will not accept the fact that our copiers are exceptional quality. He demands we reprint and/or reimburse money. He says we should have called if we could not do the quality he wanted.

Company's present position: Our photocopying is superior in the industry. When we feel our quality could have been better, we immediately make amends. When we could have done no better and the customer won't accept this, we normally offer a 10 to 15 percent discount off our published price as a goodwill gesture. That is our lowest offer. (Normally to obtain the type of quality these customers want would cost from two to five times what we charge for photocopies.)

Your Solution

_____

_____

_____

_____

IV. Joe, Quote Department

Situation: The customer calls in for a quote. When we receive the written order, we notice there will be extra charges (for example, less than a ⅛" border). Customer says she informed us of all details, so we should stick with our phone quote. She has already sent in a check.

Company's present position: We stress on the phone and in our catalogs that all phone quotes are subject to change upon receipt of the order, that all orders must be verified. Customers still insist they told you something they did not. If they are stubborn, we offer to split minor differences in the spirit of good customer relations. If the amount is quite large, we give them a small percentage discount.

Your Solution

_____

_____

_____

_____

_____

V. Mona, Order Desk Clerk

Situation: Telling customers their labels will take from five to ten working days, when they insist they need them tomorrow at the latest!

Company's present position: Our catalog states:

> Turnaround time: Normal turnaround time is five working days (not including UPS transit time). We're the fastest in the industry! To save still more time, special UPS two-day or UPS one-day service—at your cost. Long runs (over 10,000), two-color, special sizes, bleed, weatherproof labels, tint, PMS match, singles, screens, allow two weeks.

Notice we don't guarantee anything. We do not often accept "special" rushes in order to protect our other orders in-house from becoming late. If we cannot offer a "rush," our other alternative is to offer an "order status" call the day before or the day of requested shipping. At this time, we advise the customer whether the order has been shipped or has a projected ship date. The customer can then tell us whether to ship express.

(continues)

Worksheet 4 (*continued*)

Your Solution

_____

_____

_____

_____

_____

VI. Dottie, Order Desk Clerk

Situation: Having to advise the customer he does not qualify as a wholesale dealer and having to then quote retail (50 percent more).

Company's present position: We are very aggressive in protecting our dealer base by qualifying each new dealer's eligibility to receive wholesale pricing. We in no way wish to undercut our dealers and be accused of taking away their customers. Individuals can order from our catalog. Catalog prices are the same as our dealers charge, so if customers have never ordered through our dealers, we offer to sell to them at the retail price, no matter how large their order. To qualify as a dealer, the customer must be in the printing trade and offer the labels for resale.

Your Solution

_____

_____

_____

_____

_____

VII. Janet, Switchboard Operator

Situation: Having to tell people they can't call on the toll-free line to place a stamp order.

Company's present position: We accept stamp orders only through the mail and on our local line. The toll-free line is reserved for label orders. We did a cost-benefit analysis and concluded that we couldn't afford to take stamp orders this way, even though we risk losing some customers.

Your Solution

_____

_____

_____

_____

_____

VIII. Janet, Switchboard Operator

Situation: Discouraging an angry customer who has already talked to the customer service department (or wants to bypass it) and wants to talk to the owner, president, or manager.

Company's present position: Our customer service department is definitely the place for the customer to get the fastest and best solutions to problems. Customer service representatives (CSRs) know the system and many times are already familiar with the problem. When customers try to bypass this department, the problem normally takes longer to solve. We have a customer service supervisor who is available to talk with the customer when the CSR has run out of ideas. In ninety-nine cases out of a hundred, upper management will uphold the supervisor's decision. Upper management will occasionally take a call if a customer is irate. If we spoke to every customer who wanted to talk to us, we would not be able to do our jobs! (Many times customers pretend to be angry just to talk to senior management, because they think they'll get a better deal. These are the people we most discourage from talking to upper management.)

Your Solution

_____

_____

_____

_____

_____

Reprinted by courtesy of Learning Dynamics, Inc.

Keys to Customer-Driven Service

Based on our experience and the experience of the most successful companies in our survey, we have distilled the following key components of customer-driven service:

1. Get top management commitment and involvement in customer satisfaction.
2. Assess strengths and barriers to customer commitment. Where are you?
3. Establish regular contact with customers to learn and meet their needs, expectations, and requirements.
4. Set visible performance measurements and goals.
5. Establish customer-driven policies, strategies, and systems.
6. Commit managers to new customer-driven culture; train in new roles.
7. Build employee motivation, commitment, and self esteem.
8. Empower and train Customer-Champions at all levels.
9. Solve problems and continuously improve.
10. Establish feedback systems to and from employees to gain their participation and ideas.
11. Recognize, reward, and celebrate achieving performance goals.
12. Evaluate and continuously improve progress.

The customer commitment survey that follows (Worksheet 5) helps you rank your organization on these dimensions. Chapters 6 through 17 will show you how to initiate and integrate these strategies in your operation.

Worksheet 5. Customer Commitment Survey

Directions: To evaluate your organization's culture on the key factors in customer-driven service, rate the statements below on the following scale:

$$1 = \text{Never}$$
$$2 = \text{Rarely}$$
$$3 = \text{Sometimes}$$
$$4 = \text{Usually}$$
$$5 = \text{Always}$$

Then complete your Profile Index at the end of the evaluation.

Customer Orientation	*Circle Your Rating*
1. Taking care of our customers is a top priority in our organization—more important than costs.	1 2 3 4 5
2. We "listen" carefully to our customers' needs through our informal feedback systems and act on this information.	1 2 3 4 5
3. We have a formal process in place to determine our customers' wants, needs, and expectations, now and for the future.	1 2 3 4 5
4. When we lose a customer we know why. Or we find out.	1 2 3 4 5
5. Our repeat business exceeds the industry average.	1 2 3 4 5
6. Our day-to-day activities are in harmony with our values and goals about customer satisfaction.	1 2 3 4 5
7. My managers' concerns and activities have convinced me that customer care is important.	1 2 3 4 5
8. Our customers have advocates in our organization.	1 2 3 4 5

Management Climate	*Circle Your Rating*
1. Our managers "walk what they talk."	1 2 3 4 5
2. The predominant attitude around here is risk-taking rather than defensive.	1 2 3 4 5
3. Managers give workers the responsibility and authority to take care of customers.	1 2 3 4 5
4. People think "competition" means other companies, not the person down the hall.	1 2 3 4 5
5. We see ourselves as customers and suppliers in our work relationships with each other.	1 2 3 4 5

(continues)

Worksheet 5 (*continued*)

Cooperation/Integration	*Circle Your Rating*
1. People at all levels can participate in decision making.	1 2 3 4 5
2. Supervisors and managers in different departments work well together.	1 2 3 4 5
3. Very few things fall through the cracks because the left hand doesn't know what the right hand is doing.	1 2 3 4 5
4. Our systems make clear who has responsibility for tasks.	1 2 3 4 5
5. The organization's goals are set at the top, based on our mission, and are clear and achievable.	1 2 3 4 5
6. Results and goal achievement are rewarded both formally and informally.	1 2 3 4 5
7. We have clear measures and tracking systems to tell us how we are meeting our customers' requirements—in every department.	1 2 3 4 5

Attitude and Skills	*Circle Your Rating*
1. What happens in the organization really matters to all our people—executives and workers alike.	1 2 3 4 5
2. People feel responsible, needed, and empowered to do what needs to be done to take care of our customers and keep them satisfied.	1 2 3 4 5
3. Our customer service representatives know how to identify/solve customer service-related problems.	1 2 3 4 5
4. Problem-solving skills are used in every department and are standard operating procedure.	1 2 3 4 5
5. Our managers and supervisors have the skills to influence others, communicate effectively, and motivate and lead subordinates, particularly through periods of economic challenge and change.	1 2 3 4 5

Costs/Prevention/Results	*Circle Your Rating*
1. Our focus is on preventing problems rather than fixing them after the fact.	1 2 3 4 5
2. We regularly collect data on the costs of waste, rework, errors, and other elements of poor service quality.	1 2 3 4 5
3. We concentrate on exceptional care of customers, rather than cost-cutting, to increase our profits and earnings.	1 2 3 4 5

Scoring and Interpretation

Add your scores, and see what the total means below:

Score	*Interpretation*
113–140	Your corporate culture seems very customer-oriented.
85–112	You seem personally committed to service excellence, but you need to get your systems in line.
57–84	You may recognize the importance of customers, but your organization doesn't seem to be acting this way.
28–56	You and your organization seem to be interested in other things instead of service excellence.

Reprinted by courtesty of Learning Dynamics, Inc.

Five

Customer-Driven Service: Today's Competitive Edge

Why is managing a company to meet customer needs so important?

The first reason is to differentiate your company from its competitors. A lot of products are becoming commoditylike these days. There is little to tell them apart. Think about the services and products you use: banks, utilities, insurance companies, stock brokers, hospitals, even soft drinks. Despite all advertising claims in these fields, there's not much difference between competitors' products. And prices aren't usually much different either. The main reason we choose one over another is because it better meets our needs in some way: service, ease of use, or ability to do what it promises to do.

The second reason to become customer-driven is to build market share.

As Figure 5-1 shows, over the long run, you can't maintain market share with unique features alone, because your competitors will catch you. You can increase market share only through loyal customers and excellent service.[1]

And you can't build market share by cutting price or quality. Studies show that in the long run that approach is doomed to failure.

The final reason to become customer-driven is to make your company a legend or you a hero.

Figure 5-2, based on a study conducted by a GE task force, lists the differences between businesses rated high in quality and those rated low.

The evidence is clear: To be a hero in the eyes of customers, you need to listen to what they want, and deliver it.

In summary, the point of being customer-driven is to install your customers at the heart of your operation. Then use their needs to guide all your decisions. Customers need to be at the center of all of your goals, your strategies, and your systems.

(text continues on page 45)

Figure 5-1. Contributors to market share.

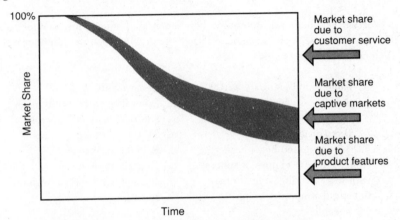

As unique product features tend to become generic through the introduction of competitive products, market share is maintained through a combination of captive markets and customer service.

Reprinted by courtesy of Learning Dynamics, Inc.

Figure 5-2. Companies rated high vs. low in quality.

High

• Emphasized real (not assumed) customer expectations.
• Identified customers' specific needs through contact research.
• Used customer-based quality performance measures.
• Established quality control systems for *all* functions.

Low

• Downgraded the customer's viewpoint.
• Thought "high quality" meant "tight tolerance."
• Expressed quality objectives as defects per unit.
• Had formal quality control only for manufacturing.

Adapted from Robert D. Buzzell and Bradley T. Gale, *The PIMS Principles* (New York: Free Press, 1987), p. 118.

Worksheet 6. What Makes Buyers Buy?

This exercise will help you determine how much you value price, service, and quality, and under what circumstances. Circle the purchase you would rather make for each of the following pairs:

1.	c.	A "name brand" milk @ $2.09	a.	Generic milk @ $1.89
2.	c.	Great coffee @ $4.00/lb.	a.	Fair coffee @ $3.90/lb.
3.	c.	$100 tires lasting 12 months,	a.	$80 tires lasting 8 months
4.	b.	$200 repair taking 1 day	a.	$150 repair taking 5 days
5.	c.	$.90 for gas rated best	a.	$.85 for average gas
6.	b.	Retail price for clothes at a store with valet parking, free alterations, gift wrapping, helpful salespeople	a.	10 percent off the same clothes at a self-service store with no amenities
7.	b.	A movie on cable with no commercials	a.	The movie on "free" TV two years later with a commercial every 15 minutes.
8.	c.	A personal computer with numerous features that's hard to learn	b.	A computer costing the same with fewer features that's easy to learn
9.	c.	Lunch at a fast-food restaurant with good food and poor service	b.	Lunch for the same price with worse food and better service
10.	c.	A great book that's difficult to buy	b.	A good book you can find at any store
11.	a.	A compact disc player costing $119 from a discount store with a bad reputation for repairs	b.	The same CD player for $189 from a store with a good reputation for repairs
12.	b.	A one-hour photo store with mediocre quality	c.	A mail-order photo service that charges the same for better quality

Count up the number of times you have circled each letter:

	a	b	c
Total	_____	_____	_____

Interpretation

The more a's you have, the more you value *price*.
The more b's you have, the more you value *service*.
The more c's you have, the more you value *quality*.

Reprinted by courtesy of Learning Dynamics, Inc.

You can test this idea on yourself as a customer by filling out Worksheet 6.

This type of research is called conjoint analysis. When you have factors that are equally attractive, you compare them in pairs to see how much of one you would give up to get another.

Questions to Consider

- When was price your deciding factor? When was quality? When service?
- Where is each one a factor in today's marketplace?
- What do the manufacturers of these products think they are selling us? How does this compare with what we buy?
- Which is most important in your industry?
- What conclusions do you draw from this?

Our Conclusions

- Other things being equal, price is the deciding factor.
- If there is not much difference in price, product quality will decide.
- If price and product quality are pretty much the same, service quality will win out. In today's crowded market, service is becoming more of a factor. As markets mature, price differences become less important, while product and service quality become more important.

Integrated Products

What does your company sell? It used to be that if you sold widgets, that's all your company was selling, and the company with the lowest price sold the most. But today's sophisticated customers look at more than price or the "generic" product. They are strongly influenced by an "enhanced" or "integrated" product.[2]

Figure 5-3 illustrates the difference.

The generic product is the "commodity" aspect of what you're selling. If customers see little difference between competitors, they will buy mostly on the basis of price. Even though your product may be more sophisticated than the competition's, if buyers *don't see* the difference, the only way you can defend market share is by cutting your price (a no-win proposition).

The enhanced product is the "quality" aspect of what you're selling. It includes features that benefit customers. If buyers think one product is "best,". they will buy it as long as there is not too much difference in

Figure 5-3.   Fighting commodity thinking.

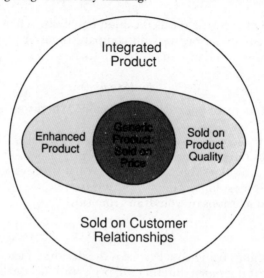

Reprinted by courtesy of Learning Dynamics, Inc.

price between it and what else is available. So if you build a better mouse-trap (or computer software or hospital), the world may beat a path to your door.

The integrated product is everything related to what you're selling. As Regis McKenna says, "It includes service, word-of-mouth references, company financial reports, the technology, and even the personal image of the CEO."[3] This is important because first, it's getting harder to make a product clearly better than your competition's, and second, buyers are more interested in these service quality aspects than they are in mere features.

For example:

Product	Generic	Enhanced	Integrated
Milk	Price	Taste	Delivery
			Packaging
			Friends' recommendations
Credit cards	Interest rate	Widespread accept-	Speed of inquiry response
	Annual fee	ance	Image
		Features (e.g., cash	Advertisements
		advances)	Insurance coverage

Fighting Commodity Thinking

Here are some examples of integrated products:

• Genentech customers (doctors) can immediately learn test results from Genentech salespeople who carry lap-top computers that provide this test data on similar patients. This technology makes Genentech's growth hormone an integrated product.

• An Atlanta parking lot has differentiated its commodity: It offers rides to airlines, bag checking, and servicing of cars while the customers travel.

• The image of Lee Iacocca is now part of the Chrysler integrated product.[4]

We believe anything can be differentiated. True, as more markets mature, it becomes more difficult, but you can do it by:

1. Avoiding commodity thinking.
2. Knowing why customers buy your product and what they do with it.

Because of the maturing and globalization of markets—product as well as service—differentiation is moving from "nice to have" to "essential for survival." Customer-driven service (and the customer relationship) is today's key differentiator. It goes beyond enhancement or product quality.

Try it for your organization. Think about the potential for integrating your product and fill in the diagram in Worksheet 7, "The Integrated Product."

Customer-Driven Differentiation

Effectively meeting customer needs requires a knowledge of customers and what they do with the product. It also requires a fair degree of imagination and the ability to place yourself in the customer's shoes.

A group brainstorming exercise will give you an opportunity to try out your skills in differentiating apparent commodities.

Brainstorming is an activity with two phases:

1. *Idea Generation.* During this phase, you select a scribe to record ideas on the flipchart. Everyone takes turns contributing as many ideas as possible. All ideas, no matter how wild, are welcome. No criticism allowed. If the group is having trouble coming up with ideas, use the "Get

Worksheet 7. The Integrated Product

Brainstorm ways to differentiate your product/service by completing the three parts of this diagram.

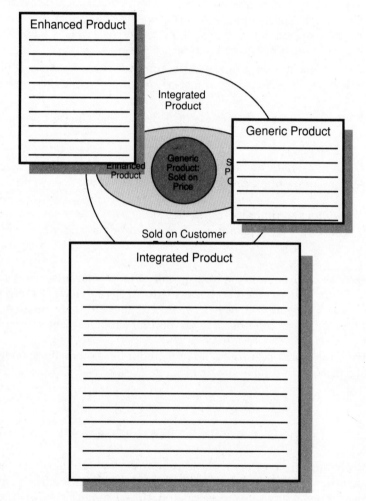

Reprinted by courtesy of Learning Dynamics, Inc.

Fired" technique: Think of an option so outrageous that you would be fired for suggesting it. That gets you unusual approaches you can build on.

2. *Idea Refinement.* When you have run out of ideas, go back and look at the list. Try to find something useful in each idea. To respond to an idea, select three things you like about it. If there are aspects of the idea you don't like, state them as concerns, not criticisms, that is, wishes you may have to improve it. Then think about how you can turn the concerns into opportunities by enhancing the original suggestion.

Now here's an activity (Worksheet 8) you can do in a group to practice integrating products.

The Service Business Plan

Before investing in a new company, you would probably ask the founder for a business plan. You'd want to make sure any would-be entrepreneurs have gone through the discipline of thinking about markets, customers, competitors, and profit margins before they are actually in the middle of things (and spending your money).

It also makes good sense for every business to prepare a service business plan on a regular basis: It's good discipline, and you need answers before crises arise. While your organization may plan product quality, few companies plan their integrated product completely.

The service business plan links marketing, differentiation strategies, and customer service with the plans for the products themselves—and with your mission statement.

The service business plan needs to answer ten questions. Review these questions and, in Worksheet 9, write the best plan you can come up with for your organization.

Here, for example, is a brief analysis of product and a service business plan for a chain of discount department stores:

The *generic product* is general merchandise sold at the lowest prices.

The *enhanced product* is reliable merchandise.

The *integrated product* is bare-bones service, a reputation for cheapness, a struggling company, and an ebullient CEO who personifies the company.

Service Business Plan

Mission:	To let everyone know that our prices are lowest.
Products:	Lowest prices, but we could beef up our service component.
Customers:	Lower-middle and working class, especially minorities and young and middle-aged women.

(*text continues on page 52*)

Worksheet 8. Integrating Products

Instructions

1. Get together with a group of four or more people.
2. Brainstorm as many strategies as you can for differentiating one of the following products:

> Paper clips
> 5 ¼" computer diskettes
> Insurance
> Twelve-ounce beverage cans
> Natural gas
> Package delivery

3. You may not change the product itself; instead, focus on the integrated product, such as delivery, customer relationship, billing, references, and value-added features.
4. When you are finished generating ideas, look over the list and try to find something useful, or something to improve on, in each.

Product:_____

Differentiation strategies:_____

_____

_____

_____

_____

_____

_____

Reprinted by courtesy of Learning Dynamics, Inc.

Where:	The Midwest. Trying to find customers with new stores in the East, but they are resisting. They buy products directly.
What they buy:	Savings. But we're not sure it's what they're still interested in.
Relationship:	Distant; little market research is done, so we're not sure how they feel.
What they do with what they buy:	Can also only be assumed.

Worksheet 9. Service Business Plan

Answer each of these questions:

1. *What is our mission statement?* (If you don't have one for your organization or department, see the next section.) The mission should be a summary of all the following points as well.
2. *What products do we produce?* What are the components of the integrated products—services, distribution, support, relationship, etc.?
3. *Who are our customers?* What are the major subgroupings of customers, or market segments?
4. *Where are our customers?* Geographically? In terms of level in their organizations? How many steps are there between us and them? How do they get our products?
5. *What do our customers buy?* How close is it to what they need? How do we know?
6. *What is our relationship with our customers?* How do we know they are getting what they need? How do they learn how to use our products?
7. *What do they do with what they buy?*
8. *Who are our known competitors?* Who else provides products or services that could be substituted for ours in the customer's eyes? Who will our competitors be tomorrow?
9. *What is it that our customers most value* about our organization (not just our products)? About our competitors?
10. *What trends are there* in our customers' businesses or lifestyles that are likely to change what they will need from us?

To write a preliminary guide to your strategy, complete the following. If you don't know an answer, write "unknown" for now.

Service Business Plan

Mission:_____

_____

Products/services:_____

_____

Customers: Who?_____

_____

Customers: Where?_____

_____

(continues)

Worksheet 9 (*continued*)

What they buy:_____

_____

Relationship:_____

_____

What they do:_____

_____

Competitors:_____

_____

What customers value:_____

_____

Trends:_____

_____

Reprinted by courtesy of Learning Dynamics, Inc.

Competitors:	K-Mart, Ames, Sears, etc.
What customers value:	Low prices and the CEO.
Trends:	Might be more single-parent and two-income families.

Customer-Driven Management Profile and Grid

Now let's examine your current management style in terms of how customer-driven you are. Fill out the Customer-Driven Management Profile that follows in Worksheet 10. Then follow the instructions to score the profile.

Here is what the four styles mean:

1. *Seekers* are interested in customer perspectives but don't come face-to-face with customers very often. They use every means available to them to gather information about customer needs and strive to make customer-driven decisions. They value service excellence highly, and they

(*text continues on page 56*)

Worksheet 10. The Customer-Driven Management Profile

In the questions below, please circle the appropriate answer number.

Note that some questions refer to the *organization*, meaning the entire company in which you are employed. Other questions refer to your *group*, or that part of the organization for which you are directly responsible.

1. In your group, the first priority is:
   a. Cost control
   b. Staying on schedule
   c. Employee morale
   d. Quality of your products/services
   e. Understanding and meeting customer needs

2. In your group, customer complaints are:
   a. Discouraged
   b. Ignored
   c. Tolerated
   d. Encouraged
   e. The basis for improvement

3. Your organization's competitive strategy is based on:
   a. Staying even with competitors
   b. Being the low cost provider
   c. Being the high value provider
   d. Finding markets and niches where there are no competitors
   e. Constantly finding out how to improve service in the customers' eyes

4. How much of your organization's business is from repeat customers?
   a. None/don't know
   b. Less than 25%
   c. 25–50%
   d. 51–75%
   e. 76–100%

5. How many of your organization's employees are rewarded or appraised based on customer-linked measures?
   a. None
   b. Less than 10%
   c. 10–25%
   d. 26–50%
   e. 51–100%

(continues)

Worksheet 10 (*continued*)

6. What percentage of the people in your group are aware of how their customers use the products/services your group provides?
   a. None
   b. 1–10%
   c. 11–25%
   d. 26–50%
   e. 51–100%

7. How often do you personally meet with customers?
   a. Never
   b. Several times a year
   c. Monthly
   d. Weekly
   e. Several times per week

8. What percent of the employees in your group are in contact with external customers at least monthly?
   a. None
   b. Less than 10%
   c. 10–25%
   d. 26–50%
   e. 51–100%

9. How often is your group the customer's first contact with your organization?
   a. None
   b. Less than 25%
   c. 25–50%
   d. 51–75%
   e. 76–100%

10. How much time do you personally spend on the phone or meeting with people who do not work for your organization?
    a. None
    b. Less than 25%
    c. 25–50%
    d. 51–75%
    e. 76–100%

The Customer-Driven Management Grid

To score the CDM Profile, first calculate your customer-driven scores:

Question Number	Score
1.	
2.	
3.	
4.	
5.	
Total	

Next, calculate your customer-contact scores:

Question Number	Score
6.	
7.	
8.	
9.	
10.	
Total	

(continues)

Worksheet 10 (*continued*)

The CDM Grid

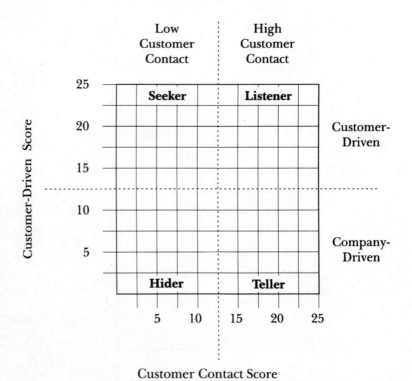

Customer Contact Score

consistently seek new and better ways of determining what customers need.

2. *Listeners* are people who have a high degree of customer contact and are customer-driven. They listen carefully to customer needs and do their best to build relationships that exceed customer expectations. When company policies conflict with customer needs, Listeners try to find win-win solutions.

3. *Hiders* have little customer contact and are glad of it. They believe that their function in the company has nothing to do with customer satisfaction, so they don't think about customers.

4. *Tellers* have a lot of customer contact, but they don't listen. They are more likely to tell a customer what the company wants him or her to do. Their goal is to see policies enforced (usually because management

values rules that meet company needs, not customer needs). Tellers have little leeway in making decisions.

Questions

- Where are you now?
- Where would you like to be ideally?
- Which quadrant do you think it's "better" to be in, if any? (You can't control low customer contact, but you can control customer-drivenness.)

Dr. Edwards Deming (considered by many to be the "father of quality") believes that a merely "satisfied" customer will go elsewhere when a competitor cuts its price. What does this say about the quadrants?

Mission Statements

If you don't yet have a mission statement, writing one is a good place to start the service quality improvement process.

If you do have one, you might want to just skip ahead to the next section. Or perhaps you might quickly review this approach to a customer-driven mission.

To provide customer-driven service, an organization needs a clear mission statement focused on customers.

Why do we consider the mission statement so important? Peter Drucker answers this best:

"Every one of the great business builders we know of—from the Medici and the founders of the Bank of England down to IBM's Thomas Watson in our day—had a . . . clear theory of the business which informed his actions and decisions." [5] In other words a mission.

A clear mission is the basis for easily understood, achievable business goals. It is the foundation for priorities, strategies, plans, and work assignments. All these require knowing "what our business is and what it should be." Domino's Pizza is an example:

Domino's Mission

To deliver a high-quality pizza, hot, within 30 minutes, at a fair price. [6]

This statement doesn't meet all of our criteria for a mission, but it is effective in guiding the company's behavior.

1. None of their restaurants has a table. Eat-in customers would interfere with their goal of speedy delivery.

2. Distribution supports their mission. They prepare basic ingredients ahead of time at regional centers and ship them every two days.
3. Menus are simple. For example, pizza comes in only two sizes.
4. Domino's designs its restaurants for maximum speed, and pizzas are made quickly as orders are phoned in.
5. Automatic oven timers and temperature controls prevent burnt pizzas.
6. Routes are planned in advance to deliver pizzas as fast as possible.
7. Crushproof boxes and insulated pouches keep pizzas warm.

As founder Tom Monaghan says, "Everything we do at this company should be toward [the mission], or we shouldn't be doing it."

One of the first formal mission statements came from Theodore Vail of AT&T eighty years ago. Believe it or not, that long ago he said:

Our business is service.[7]

At that time, most countries had government-owned telephone services. So to stay private, AT&T needed to gain community support by creating customer satisfaction.

More recently, Jan Carlzon credits publicizing his mission with helping in his startling turnaround of SAS Airlines. He says he was "able to stir new energy simply by ensuring that everyone connected with SAS—from board members to reservation clerks—knew about and understood our overall vision."[8]

To define a business mission, there is only one starting point. It is the customer. The customer defines the business.

A business is not defined by the company's name or articles of incorporation. It is defined by the want the customer satisfies upon buying a product or a service. To satisfy the customer is the purpose of every business.

To write a mission statement, start by answering these questions about your customers:

Customer-Focused Mission Questions

1. *Who is the customer?* Sometimes there are many customers. For example, a bank has depositors and borrowers; each group has different needs, but the bank must satisfy both to stay in business.

Hotels' customers are both corporations (those who book conferences, group tours, etc.) and individual guests.

Vail of AT&T noted the following eighty years ago: The phone company's customers were both its subscribers and the state regulatory agencies who could make or break it.[9]

2. *Where is the customer?* In some companies, you have to know where your customer is to define your mission. Sears realized this in the 1920s when it discovered its farm base was beginning to move to town. Sears recognized that store location was an important decision twenty years before other retailers.[10]

Bankers who answered this question in the 1950s realized that their customers were becoming multinational and located branches abroad.

Although "where" has declined in importance for a great many industries, those serving local communities and certain types of localities (like Urban Outfitters, which specializes in "city" clothes) had better understand demographics.

3. *What does the customer buy?* Take Cadillac, for example. Cadillac weathered the depression by answering that question. Who are Cadillac's competitors, and what need does the Cadillac buyer really want to fill?[11] Cadillac does not compete with Chevy or Honda. It does compete with Lincoln, BMW, and Infiniti. And it also competes with diamonds and minks. Cadillac shoppers don't buy transportation, they buy status.

4. *What is value to the customer?* Customers don't buy services or products. They buy satisfaction of wants. They buy value. For example, a successful European company sells electronic components from many different manufacturers, usually at a higher price than ordering direct. If someone needs a part, the company knows what different parts can fulfill the function and supplies them the same day. Expertise and speedy service equal value to their customers, who are willing to pay a premium. "Our business is not electronic parts, it is information," says the founder.[12]

Once you've defined your customer, write a mission statement that answers these three questions:[13]

1. *What function are we trying to fulfill in society?* In answering the "what" question, look beyond the services you may now perform. For example, not too many years ago, railroads would have answered this question "running trains." They didn't think in terms of "transporting people and goods," so they never got into air transportation or, later, into aerospace.

A better way to answer this "function" question is to think about the customer needs you are attempting to meet. If the railroads had answered the function question with "transporting people," they might have thought about other ways to diversify and prosper.

Or take the oil companies. Most would probably answer this question "finding and marketing oil." What is a more customer-focused way to answer this question?

The oil companies might do better to define themselves as "providing energy." That would open up new options like solar and wind power generators.

How about detergent manufacturers? How might they look beyond their present services? One possibility is from "make soap" to "help people clean their garments," which could open up possibilities like ultrasonic cleaners.

2. *For whom do we perform our function?* No organization—even the largest—can meet everyone's needs. A mission statement identifies what portion of the total market will be your primary target. In other words, segment the market. For example, you might segment your market geographically, financially, or ethnically. A kosher food business seeks different buyers from a soul food business. Each of General Motors' divisions goes after a different socioeconomic class.

For another example, how does Federal Express segment its market from the U.S. Postal Service's? The answer is economically. FedEx's customers are willing to pay a lot more than the Post Office's for guaranteed delivery.

Finally, and perhaps most importantly:

3. *How do we go about filling our function?* These answers define what sets you apart from your competitors; they provide the "why" a customer should buy from your company and not another one. It may involve a marketing strategy, such as having the lowest cost, the leading technology, the highest quality, or the best service. It may involve a distribution system, such as regional warehouses, 24-hour service, or walk-in appointments. Or it may involve a selling system like telemarketing, home parties, or mail order.

It goes without saying that to be truly successful, you need to differentiate your company from your competitors. And the best chance for a service organization is to distinguish itself as an outstanding service provider.

Once you've answered these three questions, put your mission statement into writing. This is a brief statement—100 words or less—that identifies your business.

Sample Mission Statements

The mission statement, most importantly, needs to define what sets you apart from your competitors. For example, a fast-food restaurant chain may decide:

XYZ Corporation is a low-cost provider of meals for families. We intend to maintain our position as a market leader by meeting customer needs through a high level of quality and service, while maintaining high enough earnings to satisfy our investors.[14]

Defining the company's mission in terms of "meals for families" may lead it to diversify into frozen dinners sold in supermarkets.

As you prepare to write, consider the following:[15]

- What was our purpose when we were founded?
- How does that purpose relate to today's market?
- How do we see our market in the future? Where will we fit in?
- Who are our customers now? Who would we like them to be? What do they want from us?
- What advantage can we derive from our size?
- What kind of technological edge do we have?
- What is our reputation for service?
- What are our other strengths and weaknesses?
- Who are our major competitors? What are their strengths and weaknesses?

Once you've written your first draft, critique your mission statement by answering these five questions:

1. Does your mission indicate your organization is customer-driven?
2. How can you focus more on customers?
3. If you have a mission statement now, how would you rewrite it to better focus on customers?
4. How will your department help make it happen?
5. What do you need to do as a manager?

As a manager, you have some control over your responsibility. We recommend you use it to become an island of customer-driven service.

As a start, create a departmental vision statement.

Cliff Bolster, Bath Iron Works, has written one of the best department vision statements we've seen:

- Treat every person with whom we come in contact with respect and dignity.
- Deal with the divisions we service as if they are valued customers and, if they chose to, could find another source for the services we provide.
- Demonstrate by our actions the way we want the whole company to operate.
- Minimize discussing and writing and maximize acting and doing to achieve our objectives.

Worksheet 11. Writing a Mission Statement: First Draft

1. What function are we trying to fulfill in society?
2. Whom do we perform that function for?
3. How do we go about filling that function?

Draft Statement

_____

_____

_____

_____

_____

_____

Reprinted by courtesy of Learning Dynamics, Inc.

- Take full responsibility for the quality of our department's performance and don't blame others.
- Never hear the phrase, "That's not my job."
- Give each other feedback on what we want from each other.
- Recognize achievement and celebrate success.

Here are some other departmental vision statements:

- We act as partners with our customers.
- We are committed to our customers' success, and we encourage them to teach us how to do business with them.
- We want to understand the impact of our actions on our customers.
- Our customers are as important as our stockholders.
- We exceed customers' expectations.
- We fulfill all our promises and meet every requirement.
- We choose quality over speed.
- The purpose of a sales call is to help the customer make a good decision.
- We want each employee to feel connected to our final product.
- Our people are our business.[16]

In summary, the point of a mission statement is, of course, not to determine it or write it down. The point is to clarify your goals and to guide everyone's behaviors. It needs to be at the heart of all of your plans, your strategies, your policies, and your systems. Whenever you're making a decision, use the mission statement as a fundamental input. Let it guide key decisions. It separates the important from the merely urgent. It provides a framework that supports a common strategy and achieves common objectives. Let everything you do constantly communicate and reinforce it.

Try a first draft in Worksheet 11.

Notes

1. Warren Blanding, *Customer Service Seminar Book* (Silver Spring, Md.: Marketing Publications, Inc., 1982), pp. 1–11.
2. Regis McKenna, "Marketing in an Age of Diversity," *Harvard Business Review,* September 1988.
3. *Ibid.*
4. *Ibid.*
5. Peter F. Drucker, *Management: Tasks—Responsibilities—Practices* (New York: Harper & Row, 1973).
6. "Put Your Mission Statement to Work," *Customers!* May 1987.
7. Drucker, *Management: Tasks—Responsibilities—Practices.*
8. Jan Carlzon, *Moments of Truth* (New York: Ballinger, 1987).
9. Drucker, *Management: Tasks—Responsibilities—Practices.*
10. *Ibid.*
11. *Ibid.*
12. *Ibid.*
13. Leonard Goodstein, J. William Pfeiffer, and Timothy M. Nolan, "Applied Strategic Planning: A New Model for Organizational Growth and Vitality," *The 1985 Annual: Developing Human Resources* (San Diego: University Associates, 1985).
14. *Ibid.*
15. William Christopher, *The Achieving Enterprise* (New York: AMACOM, 1974).
16. Peter Block, *The Empowered Manager* (San Francisco: Jossey-Bass, 1987).

Part II

The Twelve-Step Strategy

Six

Step 1: Top Management Commitment

Where do you begin keeping your customers for life? How do you start the customer-driven service process? Why can't you just train frontline customer contact people to be pleasant? Why must the whole organization be involved?

The road map in Figure 6-1 illustrates the "keeping customers for life" process.

Focusing an organization on customers is not just a matter of declaring a new policy. It involves strategies, systems, priorities, attitudes, and behaviors—in short, the organization's culture.

Achieving such a change demands that leaders be involved and committed: to set goals, model behavior, commit resources, and communicate to all their full support and commitment. Furthermore, leaders can't just start the process and then walk away; they have to stay involved.

Of course, you can make speeches proclaiming your commitment to service quality. You can have posters mounted all over the place. And you can make "customers for life" or "service quality" the theme of your advertising messages, which is what many companies do. These are useful—but not enough.

Yes, unfortunately it is not quick and easy—even if you implement all the things you'll learn in this book. But if you try to initiate a customer-driven service culture without your personal involvement and support, it has little chance of succeeding.

Commitment Starts at the Top

In his admirable book, *When America Does It Right,* Jay Sprechler looked at the service quality programs of fifty-six companies named most admired by *Fortune* magazine. He comments:

Figure 6-1.   Roadmap for implementing keeping customers for life.

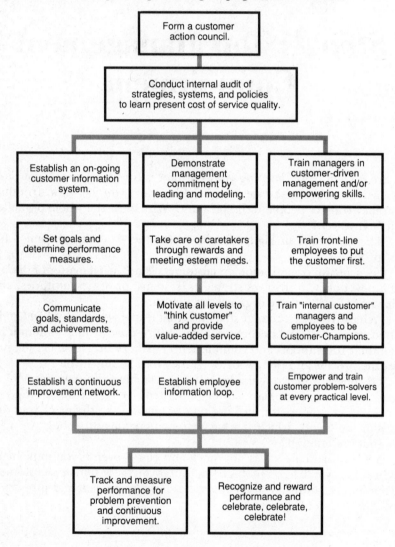

Reprinted by courtesy of Learning Dynamics, Inc.

Top level commitment is essential. . . . Service quality assurance exists at the pleasure of the policymaker—without the CEO's attention and support, service quality efforts can be neglected and wither away. . . . There isn't a single case . . . where quality developed from a bottom-up approach. It is also clear that the CEO can never walk away from maintaining a direct, highly-visible, and pervasive involvement in quality.[1]

The following examples demonstrate his point:

• Citicorp believes in using service managers to set the example for others.

For example, Citicorp Savings of California describes senior management's commitment this way:

Service excellence is a non-negotiable requirement of Citicorp Savings' strategic plan. It is no more an option for the organization than is operational control. It is an essential and uncompromisable element in our future success. It is up to every manager to actively and visibly support the achievement of service standards, and it is up to every manager to coach employees in being sensitive to service in all aspects of our business—service to our customers as well as service to each other. . . .

• Bell Atlantic is one of the regional holding companies formed in 1984, following the Bell system breakup. The managers believe, "It is the quality of a corporation's service that distinguishes it in the marketplace. Many customers base their first purchase decision on price, but they buy the second time on the basis of service."

Officers and managers are rewarded both on the basis of meeting high service standards and on financial performance. If they don't attain MPLs (minimum performance levels), rewards are reduced or eliminated.

• John J. Creedon, CEO, has been the driving force behind Met Life's "quest for quality." For example, he coined the phrase, "Quality is more a journey than a destination."

Met Life's quality credo states, "Quality is the key to our future success. Met Life customers are our first priority: Without customers, there is no reason for a business to exist. Exceeding the expectations of our customers will make Met Life 'the Quality Company.'"

• To Westinghouse, "total quality" means "Performance leadership in meeting customer requirements by doing the right things right, the first time."

Figure 6-2.   The triangle of quality.

Reprinted by courtesy of Learning Dynamics, Inc.

Total quality is crucial to survival in global competition for them, not a temporary fashionable program. Their former chairman states their mission this way:

"We are a diversified, technology-based corporation, operating globally.

Our mission is to manage our resources in ways that create value for our customers, employees, and stockholders.

We do this by managing our operations to achieve total quality in everything we do."

Westinghouse looks at total quality as a triangle; as shown in Figure 6-2.

Hospitals frequently talk "quality health care," but few know how to ask customers how they judge quality. Hospital Corporation of America believes hospitals need to move from quality assurance to measuring and improving care quality from both the external customer's and internal provider's perspective. They feel hospitals need to change to this to survive.

American Express sees quality service as its top strategic marketing weapon. Chairman Jim Robinson lists four factors that Amex's success depends on:

"Quality, Quality, Quality, and *Quality*."[2]

Both *Time* and *Fortune* magazines have praised Amex as a top service provider. Amex believes that "when it comes to quality, the power of executive leadership cannot be underestimated."[3] As *Business Week* puts it, "Quality is not evangelism, suggestion boxes, or slogans. . . . It is a way of life."[4]

What is your way of life? What do you spend your time doing? What values are you modeling? The answers to these questions are crucial because, if you hope to make the customer-driven service process work, everyone must know that *you* are behind it. Once you make it a top goal for your organization, communicate this to all of your employees with your behavior.

Let's do an exercise. Turn to Worksheet 12, "How You Spend Your Time."

Modeling the Behaviors You Want

Probably the single most important way to show your involvement and commitment to customers is to "walk what you talk"—to model your behavior values for your subordinates. (You can't just *set* values or *talk* values. You have to *do* values.)

As a manager, the most irreplaceable resource you have is time. You spend your time doing what you value. If your subordinates see that you are committed to service quality and meeting customer requirements, see you visiting field offices, talking to or otherwise caring for customers, this is what they will value and imitate.

Using the Laws of Human Behavior

In all life situations, behaviors are learned from past experiences: conversations, sights, events, sounds, and smells, all of which identify the conditions under which a behavior will be rewarded, ignored, or punished.

So it is with your staff. At meetings, for example, they soon learn that when you say, "Okay, that's it," it's appropriate to leave. In the absence of that statement, they learn that leaving your office is not a very good idea.

We all learn these complicated cues quite simply. By responding to some, we find ourselves rewarded, while responses to others are ignored or punished. And this is a key factor in how your people will know whether you are really committed to customers or just giving it lip service.

Worksheet 12. How You Spend Your Time

To determine what kind of message you are sending to subordinates about how much you value customer care, estimate how many hours in the average week you spend doing each of the following:

_____ 1. Personally serving customers
_____ 2. Cutting costs
_____ 3. Visiting offices in the field
_____ 4. Talking to other executives, managers, etc.
_____ 5. Finding out what your customers, ex-customers, and non-customers want
_____ 6. Talking to stockholders
_____ 7. Learning what customers think of your service
_____ 8. Making technical improvements
_____ 9. Recognizing employees who provide excellent care
_____ 10. Planning and scheduling

Scoring

A. Total for odd-numbered items (1, 3, 5, 7, 9)   _____
B. Total for even-numbered items (2, 4, 6, 8, 10)   _____

Interpretation

Your "A" total is the time you spend on customer care. Your "B" total is the time you spend on activities unrelated to customer care. If your "A" total is higher, you are sending a message to your subordinates that you value customer care.

Reprinted by courtesy of Learning Dynamics, Inc.

The second law of behavior is extremely relevant: At work, as in the outside world, behavior that is followed immediately by a reward is likely to be repeated. When you tell a subordinate, "Jane, you handled that upset customer really well. You were sympathetic and concerned. I wish everyone did as well. Keep up the good work!" Jane (and everyone else who heard you) is far more likely to be sympathetic to upset customers in the future than if you just took her for granted.

In behavioral language, such immediate rewards are called *positive reinforcements,* and these rewards strengthen and increase behavior. These positive reinforcements can take many forms: material things, like money, jewelry, club membership dues, or an ice cream sundae; or activities like travel, professional development workshops, or a special lunch.

They can be intangible rewards like being invited somewhere, being promoted or, especially, receiving praise, respect, and recognition.

Another law that is extremely relevant is: Behavior that is followed immediately by punishment is less likely to occur again. When you use any form of punishment (put downs, open criticism, or loss of pay), you have a powerful impact on behavior—and a lasting one. And, unfortunately, you may not even know that your organizational policies and systems are imbedded with punishments.

Bell South is an example. A Learning Dynamics, Inc. (LDI) staff consultant had attempted for some time to improve telephone operators' customer satisfaction ratings. But the operators resisted all attempts to be more helpful and less abrupt with customers. Then he discovered that a company policy (so old that management had forgotten it was on the books) decreed that operators' salaries were docked for any amount over "average time" spent on the line.

What You Reward Is What You Get

Suppose you announce that you are committed to customers. But in your day-to-day actual behavior, you ignore or avoid customers. If employees believe that your behavior exemplifies the way to advance in your company, they will do as you do.

Let's further suppose that you base rewards (praise, bonuses) to employees on the number of customers served. Behavioral science tells us that the behavior you reward is the behavior you'll get. So if your people are rewarded for serving customers quickly, they'll try to hustle each customer along. They'll avoid answering questions and attending to special requests—the services that customers value highly.

What are some of the ways you can demonstrate your commitment to customers?

Some ideas:

• Commit resources to the goal—time, personal attention and money. Bill Knowles, chairman of National Westminster Bank, does this by addressing internal and external groups on the need for service quality and appearing in the company's video magazine and newspaper. Knowles has remained highly visible. He started the company's quality improvement program with speeches at "It's Only a Beginning" parties. And he closely monitors progress with quarterly meetings with each executive vice-president. When NatWest began a warranty program with cash payouts to customers, Knowles addressed every employee at another series of parties, detailing the program, previewing the ad campaign, and personally asking for everyone's support.

• Develop customer-friendly strategies and systems to help drive behavior. TRW's independent customer service division does this by letting authorized customers dial into the on-line technical information system that its own technicians use.

• Reward those who provide excellent service. From beer bashes to elegant dinner parties, celebrate your achievers. Give public recognition, as well as tangible rewards, to those who meet your goals. American Express Company's travel-related services division awards lunches, pins, certificates, and T-shirts to outstanding performers.

• Communicate your commitment in every publication. Incorporate it in your advertising and recognize outstanding performers in publications like newsletters and annual reports (which Hershey Foods does).

• Encourage feedback from employees and publicize and reward their successful ideas for improvement.

• Spend time with customers yourself. If you are a senior manager, insist that your key reports do the same.

• If you are the CEO, get behind it publicly. Henry Ford II did this when he gave his valedictory address to Ford's top 500 managers; it was not on the economy, products, or future prospects, but on Ford's mission of making customers the focus of everything they do.

• Disney World is another interesting example. If executives see a cigarette butt or litter on the ground, they pick it up.[5] This is how they model that cleanliness in the park is a top priority.

• Make service quality and customer satisfaction a key part of the agenda at meetings. Spend at least as much time discussing them as you do costs, production, planning, schedules, and innovation. (Citicorp reviews service performance as often as it reviews financial results.) Consider placing "customers" at the top of the agenda permanently.

• Make customer satisfaction a part of your annual meeting. At *USA Today,* the head of customer service reports results at the annual get-together with parent company executives just as the CFO does.

• Make your measurement process highly visible; keep it out front all the time. But two warnings:

1. Be sure you measure and reward what's really important and what supports your goals.
2. Don't misuse measurement. That is, don't emphasize quantity over quality.

When GTE started its quality improvement program, it faced tough sledding because employees noticed their managers' words did not match their deeds. (All managers, beginning with the chairman and his staff, had to be trained before the program worked.)

100 Percent as a Goal

Most important: Make RIGHT THINGS RIGHT 100 PERCENT OF THE TIME a goal. If you allow for errors, chances are you'll get them. Suppose you're trying for only 99 percent accuracy. You may think that would be great, but if you have just ten steps in a process and each one is 99 percent accurate, by the time you're finished, you have only 99 × 99 × 99 × 99 . . . or 90 percent accuracy. If you have one hundred steps, you're only 36 percent accurate by the time you finish multiplying the *99*s. And by the way, if you think 1 percent in itself isn't much, remind yourself that the difference in DNA (genetic code) between human beings and chimps is only 1 percent! So if your DNA were 1 percent off, you could be climbing trees![6]

Customers represent 100 percent inspection. Manufacturing organizations may check 1 percent, 2 percent, or 10 percent of their products to measure conformance to specifications.

Service organizations may have supervisors monitor every tenth customer contact to check that their people are up to snuff.

But nothing escapes your customers' notice. If something goes wrong, they'll know about it; they'll tell their friends; maybe they'll even tell you. That's why you want to be 100 percent mistake-free 100 percent of the time. Impossible? Think about it this way.

Other fields demand 100 percent. For example, we don't expect nurses to drop 10 percent of newborn babies. We don't excuse people giving us the wrong change 5 percent of the time.

Your organization is probably achieving "100 percent right" in other areas. Payroll, for example, probably rarely makes a mistake. People naturally consider their paychecks important and think payroll mistakes indicate the organization doesn't care. So payroll people take pains to be accurate.

You probably demand 100 percent of yourself in private life. You don't get lost driving home and end up at the wrong house part of the time. You don't expect you'll miss 99 percent of the other cars on the road and hit only 1 percent. You expect 100 percent in these areas, and you can do the same with your organization's customers.

In summary, by far the most important way to communicate your commitment is your behavior—how you spend your time, the behaviors you model, the goals you set, the ways you reward performance, and the messages you send with your verbal and nonverbal communications. And if you are tempted to think you don't have time, or that you have more important things to do, then keep in mind Jan Carlzon's SAS story: from an $8 million loss to a $71 million profit in about two years. What can you do with your time to top that?

Notes

1. Jay Sprechler, *When America Does It Right* (Norcross, Ga.: Industrial Engineering and Management Press, 1988).
2. Sprechler, *When America Does It Right*, p. 106.
3. *Ibid.*
4. Otis Port, "Quality," *Business Week*, June 8, 1987, p. 134.
5. Karl Albrecht and Ron Zemke, *Service America* (Homewood, Ill.: Dow Jones-Irwin, 1985).
6. Philip B. Crosby, *Quality Without Tears* (New York: McGraw-Hill, 1984), Ch. 8.

Seven

Step 2: Internal Evaluation

In any major business decision, good results start with goal planning and design. In designing a customer-driven service strategy, this means first learning what you are (and are not) doing now that will drive or impede your service improvement process. So Step 2 in the strategy is an internal evaluation of key areas in your organization to establish measurements and to determine:

1. The key causes of unmet customer needs and poor service quality. These causes can range from policies, systems, and unhappy employees to squirrels nibbling on the wires. But they are expensive, and you need to find them.

For example, Florida Power & Light found 60,000 billing errors yearly "requiring added man-hours of telephone traffic with customers, new billings and added postage, not to mention customer irritation." By identifying the factors contributing to the errors, FPL cut them nearly to zero.[1]

2. The internal causes of customer complaints, customer turnover, lost good will, damaged reputation, employee turnover, and "hidden" costs, like lawsuits and design errors. For example, Winnebago found that dealer warranty expenses—both high and low—represented internal, although different, problems.[2]

3. The total cost—in dollars wasted and employees' time—of rework, correcting errors, collecting overdue receivables, and other problems caused by poor service. Incidentally, studies show that in the average company, these costs run between 15 percent and 30 percent of gross income. So they are well worth looking for.

4. The benchmark information you need for goal-setting improvement strategies and for measuring progress.

5. The best strategies for creating your action plan to gain organizational commitment to customer satisfaction 100 percent of the time.

Some people feel that service is intangible and therefore impossible to evaluate quantitatively and/or qualitatively. So you might get resistance to an evaluation. To help you, we've developed the process for evaluating service performance shown in Figure 7-1.[3] Notice how this approach can apply to measuring service in any organization.

Now let's examine each aspect of auditing service quality mentioned in Figure 7-1.

• *Strategy.* Are people doing the right things?

For example, if a businessman comes into a bank seeking a loan, does the banker treat him like a customer? Or does the banker treat him like a bandit or talk down to him?

You can specify certain behaviors in your training programs (such as stand up, offer a handshake, call the customer "Mr./Ms."), and then evaluate behavior by seeing if the banker conforms to procedures.

• *Execution/process.* Are people doing right things right?

This means following an established process to meet customers' requirements. This is more difficult than it sounds because it doesn't mean blindly following a process or system no matter what. Meeting customers' requirements always has top priority.

For example, hospitals often have a prescribed and rigid way to admit patients: getting information on name, medical insurance, and vital statistics, showing to room, issuing gown, etc. Many admissions people stick doggedly with this system, even though patients are seriously ill or need emergency treatment.

Even if you are there only for X-rays, you may go through the entire admissions and insurance routine. You get sent to the X-ray department, only to be told the technicians have gone for the day. Wait—It gets worse. You ask for your stamped, approved X-ray paper back so you can use it tomorrow. Sorry; it's only good for today. This is a true story, believe it or not.

Obviously, such dreadful treatment of patients puts the needs of the system ahead of the needs of the customers and is poor "process"—to put it politely.

To do right things right means:

1. Defining customer requirements.
2. Turning these requirements into specifications.
3. Identifying key indicators that you can track to learn which requirements are met and which are not met. You need to know whether the system is capable of meeting requirements and specifications or if it needs changing.

Often doing right things right demands empowering your service delivery people to make a decision to scrap the process and take care of the customer—in situations such as hospital emergencies, for one example. But almost all services can be monitored through your specifica-

Figure 7-1. Auditing service quality and readiness to change.

Strategy

Doing the right things

Execution/Process

Doing the right things right

Structure

Facilities/tools/technology

Design

System

Hiring/training

Quality goals

Outcomes

Results continually measured

Impact

Long/short-range effects on customers/employees

Reprinted by courtesy of Learning Dynamics, Inc.

tions and through key indicators such as: Are guests checked out within ten minutes? How many people are waiting on line to cash checks, pay bills, purchase merchandise? How many times does the aircraft arrive on time? How long does it take to correct errors, fix the problem, get credit cleared, do whatever it is that customers want done?

You can track performance by monitoring service people interacting with customers. You can also do role playing or hold drills like mock hurricanes, floods, fires, or other disasters. These will give you slices of behavior in which you can see if people are following the prescribed process and if that process is reasonable.

• *Structure.* Are facilities, tools, and technology conducive to superior work? Do the organizational systems serve customers and facilitate superior service? Are hiring and training procedures effective? Are the goals for customer care and service known by all and clearly visible?

For example, if you have automatic teller machines, are their menus in a language that local customers understand? Citicorp's are, offering English, Spanish, and Chinese in appropriate neighborhoods.[4]

One way to measure structure is to record how long your service cycle is, from the first contact with the customer to the time your product or service is in the customer's hands. Another is to see what percent of time your people are busy. You can assess quality by going through the service cycle yourself (seeing how long it takes your own order to arrive, for example).

• *Outcomes.* Are the results of the process continuously examined and measured?

In express delivery, satisfactory results means that packages arrive on time. You further measure results by looking at, say, how many packages are damaged or lost in transit. Regardless of how these rates compare to competitors, your goal is 100 percent success in having packages arrive on time and intact.

If you're a retail chain manager assessing service quality, you would time check-out lines, monitor how well stocked your shelves are, and inspect for cleanliness.

Another way to assess outcome is to ask the service people how satisfied they are with the service they are producing. Ask too if they can recommend ways to improve results. They know what kind of a job they are doing. If they trust you, and if you are meeting their esteem needs through an effective reward system, they'll tell you.

• *Impact.* What are the short- and long-term effects of service on people, that is, your customers and your employees? Let's look at the effects on your customers first.

An investment management service looks at results of clients' transactions. A training company measures how much on-the-job performance skills have improved. An advertising agency assesses whether clients' market recognition has increased. A telephone company tracks customer satisfaction ratings. And every organization can measure how long customers continue to do business with it and if reorders are increasing or declining.

You may not be able to improve all outcomes in the short term, but if you're providing superior service, these measures will improve in the long run.

There are several reliable measures of impact on your employees. Begin by defining what behaviors you are rewarding, because what you reward is what you get. Standardized employee surveys are available to help. You evaluate attitudes, concerns, and criticisms—all of which have a very direct relationship to esteem needs, job satisfaction, and quality of customer service. Finally, you can listen—really, carefully listen—to what your people are saying and how they are feeling. This will probably tell you more about how your customers are being cared for and the kind of service and quality you provide than any other measure you can take. And it doesn't cost a dime.

When Captain Eddie Rickenbacker was president of Eastern Airlines, he demonstrated the impact of poor service to top management.

Baggage handling had deteriorated badly on Eastern, and nothing he had done improved it. So Rickenbacker called a meeting of his top managers in a hot Miami hotel without air conditioning.

When the managers checked in, Rickenbacker had the desk clerks tell them their bags would be brought to their rooms. But the bags were locked in a storage area instead. The managers arrived for the next morning's meeting mostly unshaven, with unbrushed teeth and dirty clothes.

The baggage remained "lost" all day. Finally it was delivered at 3 A.M., with pounding on the doors.

On the second morning, Rickenbacker said, "Now you know how the customer feels when you mishandle his luggage!"[5]

Businesses, governments, and nonprofit organizations can all use this approach to measure service quality, because no matter what you do, you have strategy, execution, structure, outcome, and impact.

Completing Worksheet 13 will help you apply this approach to your organization.

Calculating Your Cost of Service Quality

What does service quality really cost?

Three factors comprise the total cost of service quality: preventing mistakes, monitoring performance, and fixing errors.

The "10-100-1000" rule illustrates the cost of internal failure versus external failure.

Once upon a time, quality control people would inspect a manufactured widget before it left the plant. Sometimes they'd find a mistake on the line, and it would cost, say, $10 to fix.

Other times the faulty widget would get to the door or to the distributor and be sent back for repairs, and it would cost ten times as much—$100 to fix.

Still other times, it got to customers and turned into a complaint, a recall, or, in today's environment, a lawsuit. And these mistakes would cost at least $1,000—or one hundred times the cost of finding mistakes early. So it makes sense to invest in preventing and monitoring.

Figure 7-2 illustrates this.

Prevention costs include such factors as improvements in the system that free people to do things right, and research to learn your customer requirements.

Monitoring costs include training people to check their own work and having supervisors observe service delivery.

Fixing costs include: time spent doing work over, including clerical time; rechecking work unnecessarily; wasted material and scrap; work

(text continues on page 84)

Worksheet 13. Service Quality Audit

Following are measurable areas of impact. Answer the following questions to audit how they apply to your organization:

Strategy

Are people doing the right things?

_____

_____

_____

Execution/Process

Are people doing right things right?

_____

_____

_____

Structure

Are facilities, tools, and technology conducive to superior work?

_____

Do the organizational systems serve customers, not just the organization?

_____

Do the organizational systems facilitate superior service?

_____

Are hiring and training procedures effective?

_____

Are there visible goals for pursuit of quality?

_____

Outcomes

Are the results of the process continually examined and measured?

_____

_____

_____

Impact

What are the short- and long-term effects of the service on people: customers and employees?

_____

_____

_____

Reprinted by courtesy of Learning Dynamics, Inc.

Figure 7-2. A 10-100-1000 rule.

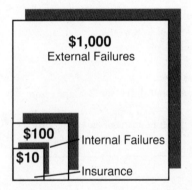

Insurance (Prevention Costs) ($10)	Protects Against:	
	Internal Failures Costs ($100)	External Failures Costs ($1,000)
• Group leadership training	• Mistakes and rework	• Lost customer and
• System improvement	• Low morale	market share
• Customer information	• Pricing and billing errors	• Customer returns
studies	• Time wasted	• Excess field service
• Empowerment with	• Excess inspection/	• Angry customers telling
problem-solving skills	supervision	10+ other people
	• Premium delivery	• Bad press
	• Excess overtime	• Poor word-of-mouth
	• Unnecessary turnover	• Lawsuits
	• Overdue receivables	• Lost repeat business
	• Resources squandered	• Lost competitive edge
	• Productivity decreased	• Poor image

Reprinted by courtesy of Learning Dynamics, Inc.

Worksheet 14. Fixing Costs

Fixing costs are expenses for doing things over that were not done right the first time. The following events may result from not doing things right the first time. Check the items that apply to your organization and ask your accounting department to calculate costs (such as time, overhead, and materials):

_____ Doing work over
_____ Rechecking work unnecessarily
_____ Wasted material and scrap
_____ Repairs for products under warranty
_____ Handling complaints
_____ Rewriting manuals and procedures
_____ Redesigning forms
_____ Overtime to fix things
_____ Underbilling
_____ Customers paying incorrect bills late
_____ Premium shipping and express delivery
_____ Sales not closed due to lack of follow up
_____ Liability insurance and claims
_____ Downtime
_____ Extra time spent with suppliers
_____ Lack of clarity on your part that induces customer errors
_____ Reentering data
_____ Your service costs (legal, telephone, postage)

Other: _____

_____

_____

Reprinted by courtesy of Learning Dynamics, Inc.

done while products are under warranty; time spent handling complaints; rewriting manuals and procedures; and your service costs, such as additional service calls, legal, telephone, postage, and express delivery.

There are three reasons for calculating the cost of quality service:

1. It gives you a baseline to measure improvement.
2. It gets people's attention. Numbers like these convince accountants; stockholders prick up their ears. And if you convince rank-and-file employees that these dollars are coming out of their bonus checks and raises, you'll have their attention too.
3. It allows you to pinpoint the most productive opportunities for improvement.

Figure 7-3.   Fixing costs iceberg (average 15 to 30 percent of gross sales).

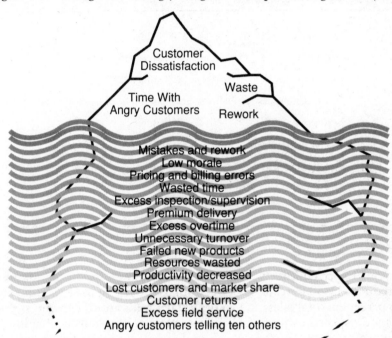

Customer
Dissatisfaction

Waste

Time With
Angry Customers   Rework

Mistakes and rework
Low morale
Pricing and billing errors
Wasted time
Excess inspection/supervision
Premium delivery
Excess overtime
Unnecessary turnover
Failed new products
Resources wasted
Productivity decreased
Lost customers and market share
Customer returns
Excess field service
Angry customers telling ten others

Reprinted by courtesy of Learning Dynamics, Inc.

Even though you are the boss, you need to sell this idea. So be as objective as possible. Have your accounting department work with you to assess your costs. Their input helps ensure that people will accept the figures as unbiased.

We've made some fixing costs suggestions in Worksheet 14. Check the items that apply to you. Give Accounting the items you want included and let them calculate the costs involved.

Fixing costs are like the iceberg in Figure 7-3. The obvious costs are above the surface, like wasted time, scrap, and doing things over. As you dig below the surface, you'll find items like overtime, absenteeism, shutdowns, accidents, insurance, lawsuits, and more, which stem from not doing things right the first time.

Typically, not much money is spent on prevention. More is spent on monitoring, and most is spent on fixing. Implementing the 12-step strategy results in spending more on prevention, spending less on monitoring, and a lot less on fixing. But what does it do to your bottom line? The

Figure 7-4.   Expected effects.

Revenue:	$500 million
Net Profit:	$50 million (10 percent)
Cost of Quality:	$125 million (25 percent)
Goal: Reduce cost of quality from 25 percent to 20 percent	
Savings:	$25 million
Cost of Improvement:	$2 million
New Net Profit:	$73 million

Return on Investment:
For every $2 invested
$23 return (1,150 percent)

Reprinted by courtesy of Learning Dynamics, Inc.

chart on "Expected Effects," Figure 7-4, shows how wasted expenditures are reduced by 50 percent or more. Suppose your cost of service quality is 25 percent of total sales, and your pre-tax profits are 10 percent. If you can cut these costs by just a fifth, down to 20 percent, look at what it will do to profits: *That 5 percent cut will go directly to the bottom line, increasing profits by half, from 10 percent to 15 percent.* If you wanted to increase profits that same 5 percent through increased sales, you would have to increase volume by 50 percent!

Figure 7-5 outlines some of the common sources of service problems.

What about you? How much of your time is spent on fixing costs?

To audit yourself, we suggest you use Worksheet 15 to keep track of your time for a week and then calculate how much of it is spent in each area.

Creating Your Action Plans for Customer Satisfaction 100 Percent of the Time

There are basically two kinds of things you can do: right things and wrong things. By right things, we mean things that serve the customers and meet their requirements. Wrong things create problems or do not help customers. (In process analysis, these wrongs are defined as non-value activities, such as rework, correcting mistakes, inspection, storage.)

Further, there are two basic ways you can perform your duties, the

(*text continues on page 90*)

Figure 7-5. Common sources of service problems.

Symptoms	*Causes*	*Possible Solutions*
1. Human		
• High turnover • "It's not my job" • Poor service • Numerous second requests • Lack of courtesy	• Lack of standards • No accountability • No rewards for good service • Priorities unclear	• Revise job description • Appraise people on customer satisfaction • Reward people for good service • Make service standards clear
2. Developmental		
• Improper responses • Inefficient investigations • Employees alienated • Employees not listened to	• Improper training • No rewards • No career paths	• Train employees in importance of customer and complaint handling • Cross train • Reward desired behavior
3. Structural		
• Misdirected calls • Complaints not responded to • Employees saying others aren't doing their jobs • Nobody knows whom problems should be referred to • Surprises	• Roles not clearly defined • Conflicting missions • People not given enough power	• Centralized contact point • Ombudsman • Coordinated goals • Decentralized authority • Team building
4. Measurement		
• Too much attention paid to irrelevant factors • Nothing done to increase customer satisfaction • No accountability • Customer satisfaction not measured • Data slow/unusable	• Customer satisfaction not measured effectively	• Tracking system for customer satisfaction and complaints • Measurement focused on behavior

(continues)

Figure 7-5 (*continued*)

Symptoms	Causes	Possible Solutions

5. Support and Communication System

• Inadequate capacity • Callers don't get through • Too much downtime • Large mail backlog • Customers call twice for same problem	• Database not integrated • Systems not user-friendly • Too much paperwork • Poor follow-up system	• Upgrade support system so first contact can resolve 95 percent of problem immediately

6. Analytical Systems

• Much time spent on fighting fires • No data on why people patronize • No data on transactions	• No prevention system • No information on root causes	• Get contact data from each location • Continually track transactions • Analyze trends

7. Design and Strategy

• Frequent customer complaints that services don't meet their needs	• Lack of research • Lack of training • Contact people don't support company policies • Designs that please other departments instead of customer	• Get input from service people before designing service package • Departments review each other's activities

8. Implementation

• New crusades every quarter • Goals conflict • Programs run out of steam too soon	• Lack of strategy • No planning	• Focus on how to satisfy customers • Limit number of new programs

9. Internal Communication

• Customers given wrong information • Contact people can't explain policies • Contact people get news from customers • Employees look dumb to customers	• Not enough time to communicate • No feedback • No timely written communication • Employees think management does not care	• Survey employees • Employee newsletter • Hold staff meetings on service • Employee ombudsman

Symptoms	Causes	Possible Solutions
10. External Communication		
• Unnecessary inquiries	• Failure to explain services to customers	• Customer education

Worksheet 15. Time Chart

To determine how much time you waste fixing mistakes, keep track of how you use your time hourly and classify it in one of the following four categories:

1. Productive work
2. Preventing problems
3. Making sure things are right
4. Fixing mistakes

Hour	Activity	Category
_____	_____	_____
_____	_____	_____
_____	_____	_____
_____	_____	_____
_____	_____	_____
_____	_____	_____

Total Time Worked _____

Add up the time you spend in each category and calculate percentages for each.

Category	Total	Percent
1. Productive work	_____	_____
2. Preventing problems	_____	_____
3. Making sure things are right	_____	_____
4. Fixing mistakes	_____	_____

Figure 7-6.   Right things/right way grid.

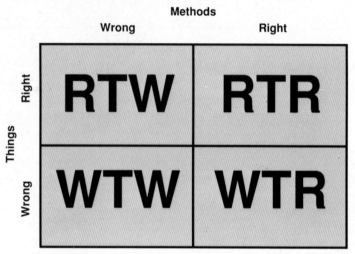

Reprinted by courtesy of Learning Dynamics, Inc.

right way and wrong way; that is, there is a correct way to accomplish your objectives and an incorrect way containing errors or based on faulty decisions.

Putting these two measures together, we can see that you can do the right things wrong, the wrong things wrong, the wrong things right, and the right things right, as we show in the grid in Figure 7-6.

Doing the wrong things the wrong way includes:

- Conducting a sloppy medical examination that was unnecessary in the first place
- Having your customers wait on line for long periods of time—and then telling them they need to go elsewhere
- Having poorly trained, indifferent, and too stressed personnel serving on your front line—anytime

Doing the right things the wrong way includes:

- Shipping perfectly grown produce too late to arrive in saleable condition
- Running great ads promising exceptional customer service and then not delivering it
- Producing a world-class product without first learning that your customers have no use for it

Doing the wrong things the right way includes:

- Infuriating customers with a superbly developed internal system
- Cutting quality to gain market share, which only works for a short time
- Reducing customer service to slash costs, which leads to a death spiral

Doing the right things the right way includes:

- Listening to customers and employees to learn and meet customer requirements
- Using state-of-the-art technology and training to reduce errors and insure customer satisfaction
- Giving customers what they want—every time

In summary, the goal of your internal evaluation is to focus commitment on doing right things right to achieve customer satisfaction 100 percent of the time. The process is your blueprint for achieving this goal and includes data collection, analysis, feedback, and planning.

Using assessment tools, one-on-one interviews, and focus groups, you assemble information on:

- Organizational strengths and weaknesses
- Obstacles and competing priorities that may impede progress
- The knowledge, skills, and attitudes of employees at all levels that will determine their contribution to improvement
- An analysis of the internal systems that drive individual and group behavior
- Your customer–supplier relationships, both internal and external
- Degree of customer orientation and commitment at all levels
- Sacred cows, myths, "get-ahead" norms, and other factors that have important impact on the success or failure of your effort

The final output is your action plan, which provides:

1. A clear vision of where you need to be
2. What needs to be done to get there
3. The specific measures you need to track improvement
4. The sequence of actions necessary to guarantee success

Notes

1. "Florida Power & Light Company," American Productivity Center, Case Study 39, 1984, Houston, Tex.: 1984.

2. Robert W. Post and Randal L. Fingarson, "Quality Service Program," in Jay Sprechler, *When America Does It Right* (Norcross, Ga.: Industrial Engineering and Management Press, 1988), p. 300.
3. James A. Fitzsimmons and Robert S. Sullivan, *Service Operations Management* (New York: McGraw-Hill, 1982), p. 371.
4. Dinah Nemeroff, "Quality in Consumer Financial Services," in Sprechler, *When America Does It Right*, p. 79.
5. "How to Create That Sense of Urgency," *Today's Leader/Manager* (Chicago: Dartnell Corp.).

Eight

Step 3: Determining Customer Requirements

Step 3 in the master strategy is to learn, and stay continually attuned to, your customers' requirements. You do this through ongoing formal and informal processes of asking questions and listening to your customers.

Superior performance—however you measure it—is a matter of meeting your customers' requirements. And you can't meet these requirements if you don't know what they are. Not what you think they are or what you want them to be, but what they really are. How do you learn what they are? Very simply, you ask your customers what they want, need, and expect, in a variety of ways. Then listen and act.

We believe that keeping customers for life demands meeting customer requirements with superior service and superior quality. However, the only people who know for sure are your customers themselves. As they say at Lockheed, "Quality will be judged by its user, not announced by its maker."[1] So in the process we advocate, we have customers tell us about their expectations and requirements.

Customers often see things differently from what managers expect. Recall our Dynamic System: Reality to customers is the way they see things. For example, a bank may have four tellers, two on window duty and two doing something else. If customers have to wait three minutes for a teller and see two of them not serving people, they will think their wait is "too long"; but if all four tellers are on window duty, customers may not get annoyed by a five-minute wait.

So to learn what customers want, ask them:

- Why they buy from you
- How they use your products and services (this might surprise you)
- What they like and dislike about you
- How you compare to competitors
- What you do that annoys, infuriates, or delights them

There are at least five types of customer insight research. The most commonly used methods follow.

Informal Research

Direct Personal Contact With Customers

Probably the most valuable, most overlooked, and least expensive method of learning what customers want is through direct personal contact. In *A Passion for Excellence,* Peters and Austin call it "managing by wandering around."[2] This means getting out of your office personally, visiting and listening to your customers instead of relying solely on computer printouts or on what subordinates tell you.

How can you learn from your customers by wandering around?

• Spend a week every few months dealing with your customers, either waiting on them, answering customer service phone calls, or making sales calls. Consider requiring all top executives to interface with customers so they know what it is like and what your people face each and every day.

A good example of the benefit of this approach is the experience of John Couch of Apple Computer, the designer who revolutionized "user friendliness." He attributes his breakthrough to working in his father's computer store every weekend while he was designing his computer:[3]

> I learned about the fears and frustrations of the average first-time computer user and the more sophisticated user. I believe it was the single most significant source of what we came up with.

• Try calling at least three customers a week and asking them how you might serve them better or how you can help correct some problems they may be having. Then listen and make notes.

Domino's Pizza calls its customers (franchisees) to check its service and product quality (response time, dough quality, etc.). It makes sure it hasn't missed anything by asking one more question, "Did we do anything that bugged you?" It summarizes answers instantly, makes them available to everyone, and bases evaluation and compensation for everyone (including the president) on the results.[4]

Another story comes from Pete Peterson, then the new president of Bell & Howell.[5] He tells how the zoom lens became a part of every home movie camera. He came across a zoom lens in a laboratory, tried it, and was amazed at what he saw. But the "experts" told him such a lens would be too expensive to offer to everyone. So he brought a lens home one evening when he was having a dinner party. He says:

> I asked everybody coming in if they wouldn't participate in a "very sophisticated piece of market research"; namely to put

the camera to their eye. To the man, the reaction was extraordinarily enthusiastic: "My, this is marvelous; I've never seen anything like this in my life." . . .

⋆ ⋆ ⋆

If more industries would try out new ideas on a low-cost basis, perhaps their expectations of what the market will bear [what customers really want] would go up.

Employee Contact With Customers

One of the best sources of information about customers is people who interface with them daily. We'll cover employee feedback in Step 10. But here are a few ideas.

• Invite customer service and salespeople's input on what customers are thinking and saying. Don't view their suggestions as "just reps swaying to every customer whim," but as the tangible rewards of listening.

• Use your repair/service personnel to learn about customers' problems. Or have nonsalespeople phone or visit customers' homes and/or offices to learn what they need.

In Chapter 14 we'll detail how Florida Power & Light saves $42 million annually by listening to contact people's reports of customer problems.[6]

Your customer contact people are an important and frequently overlooked source of knowledge about customer requirements. They have the most direct idea of what's going on, and they probably have excellent ideas of their own. Furthermore, if you bring them into the process, they'll be more motivated to participate in delivering quality service.

And don't overlook noncontact areas of the organization. Everyone in the organization has internal customers, and everyone is a customer of others in the organization. For example, your accounting department serves others in the company, so get these people to ask and report on what customers want. Simple rating systems can tell you a great deal.

We cannot overstate the value of gaining customer information on a regular basis. And more and more companies are making it a part of their standard operating procedure:

All of Apple's senior officers listen to calls on the 800 customer number. They are rewarded with "listening certificates"—and if they actually answer a call, instead of just listening, they get a gold star attached.[7]

Commtron, a videotape distributor, has established a national customer service center so that customers from any of their 25,000 retailers nationwide can have immediate access to a trained representative.[8]

A hospital equipment manufacturer asks executives to call customers six weeks after a purchase agreement. They see the benefits as:

• Letting customers know they are valued
• Uncovering problems before they reach major proportions
• Giving management a daily reminder of the real world

And customer information isn't just for executives. Encourage everyone in your organization to forward customer suggestions to you. Our experience shows that *at least half of all new service ideas, and 80 percent of new product innovations, come from customers.* So include the sales, marketing, engineering, and operations departments, and give an award for the "best idea garnered from a customer this month."

Furthermore, the competitive payoff from learning customer requirements doesn't apply just to big companies: Any size business can play and win in this game. In fact, small is easier. Take Price's Market, a convenience store, for example.

After they opened a store in Richmond, Virginia, Bob and Candy Kocher found that business was slow. They began asking those in the neighborhood who did come in, "What are you always looking for but can't get?" The overwhelming answer was unusual: "Imported beer."

The Kochers responded by stocking every kind of unusual imported beer they could find. At last report, Price's Market store is the hottest spot in town—a mob scene. Not only have Bob and Candy developed a successful local neighborhood convenience store, but people are now coming from far and wide to buy their beer. And the Kochers have plans for expansion.

There are several forms of customer research.

Formal Research

One type of formal customer information is feedback. In seeking feedback from customers, make it as easy as possible for them to tell you what they want. Enclose business reply cards with your bills. Get an 800 number, and publicize it in all your advertising.

Procter & Gamble and Lever Brothers put their 800 number on all their products. They reward those plant managers with fewest complaints on their products.

Include a feedback device somewhere in your delivery system. For example, one book publisher lists titles of books it is considering, and invites its readers to return a detachable card for more information. It knows by the number of responses which books to go ahead and publish.

Your organization can easily implement a system of collecting feedback. Your own people can gather and tabulate the data, making the system as fast and inexpensive as possible. Here are some guidelines on getting feedback from customers:

1. *Transaction-Based.* This means you ask customers to rate your service at the time they use it. For example:

- If you provide financial services, ask clients to rate your service thirty days after use.
- If you make repairs, ask customers if they are satisfied within a week after you fix their equipment.
- If you're employed by a health maintenance organization, periodically check out how you're doing with members.
- Or, if you can, use the system that many hotels use: Have customers complete a "Tell me how we've done" form and mail it directly to you.

A transaction-based system gives you more responses, which increase reliability. When it is still fresh in their mind, customers will more accurately assess your service. This feedback will serve as an early warning system, to help correct problem areas before they become disasters.

2. *Easy Response.* The less burdensome the feedback system is for customers, the more of them will use it. So make it easy to use. And pay for any postage or telephone charges involved in responding. For instance, identify up to ten attributes of your service you want customers to rate and ask for an overall measure. (Remember, use behaviors that measure satisfaction. That is, for something bought frequently, would the customer buy it again? For something bought infrequently, would he or she recommend it to a friend? For a utility, would he or she buy a related product or service?)

Figure 8-1 illustrates some sample feedback cards (comment cards distributed to customers). Notice how most answers have *five* choices. This is useful in the next step, "Ranking performance" (Figure 8-2).

To help ensure that managers and supervisors use the information customers provide, send a summary of the report for their unit the first week of each month, as in Figure 8-2, Part II. (Note how each unit is compared to company averages.) Rating of all attributes lets managers know what matters need improvement. Also, make certain you're measuring behavior the local boss can correct.)

For example, a local phone company asked customers to rank such factors as quality of reception, value received for the money, and availability of repairs. Supervisors were totally frustrated when they received

(*text continues on page 100*)

Figure 8-1. Getting feedback from customers.

1. Computer Manufacturer

Win Extra Software!

We want to know what you think!
You are the key! The information you provide will help us understand your hardware needs. Thank you for taking the time to respond.
To enter the software drawing, simply return the postage-paid reply card. We are giving away ten software packages each month. The winners may choose which one they want. Each winner will be contacted by phone.

	Strongly Agree	Agree	Neutral	Disagree	Strongly Disagree
1. The manual is well-organized.	1	2	3	4	5
2. I can find the information I want.	1	2	3	4	5
3. Instructions and lessons are easy to find.	1	2	3	4	5
4. Examples are clear and useful.	1	2	3	4	5
5. The manual, taken as a whole, is a good learning tool for the computer.	1	2	3	4	5
6. The quality of this manual would influence my purchase of software.	1	2	3	4	5

Please write additional comments, particularly if you disagree with a statement above.

Adapted from Hewlett-Packard Reader Comment Card.

2. Repair Service

Our service technician made a service call to your home on _____ and, as provided by your Maintenance Agreement, performed _____ on your _____.

It would help us evaluate our level of service if you would take a moment to fill out the following and return it in the enclosed self-addressed envelope.

	Yes	No
1. Was the service rendered on the day promised?	_____	_____
2. Was the technician neat in appearance?	_____	_____
3. Did you feel the merchandise was completely repaired?	_____	_____
4. Did the technician explain the service performed?	_____	_____

5. How long did the repair take?

    a. less than 30 minutes   _____
    b. 30–60 minutes   _____
    c. 61–90 minutes   _____
    d. more than 90 minutes   _____

Additional comments:

_____

_____

_____

Sincerely,

_____
Technical Service Manager

Adapted from Sears Roebuck & Company.

Figure 8-2.   Ranking performance.

Part I

Look at the two most important customer ratings from your comment cards (Figure 8-1). Add them together (maximum ten points). Rank your units (departments, stores, or contact people) on the ten-point scale. For example:

Rank	Unit	Score:	Three-Month	Current	Twelve-Month
1	E		9.0	9.3	8.8
2	D		8.7	8.7	8.6
3	A		8.0	7.7	8.9
4	C		7.6	7.7	7.6
5	F		6.9	7.5	6.0
6	B		4.8	5.1	5.2

Three-Month National Score: 7.5
Current Month National Score: 7.7
Twelve-Month National Score: 7.5

Part II

Give managers or supervisors a copy of the report for their unit the first week of each month. For example:

Attribute	Three-Month Branch Performance	Three-Month Company Performance
Speed	7.1	7.7
Efficiency	7.0	6.9
Friendliness	5.9	6.7
Professionalism	5.5	8.0
Overall satisfaction	6.5	7.1
Intent to repurchase	8.0	8.3

You ranked thirteenth out of fifteen branches during this reporting period.

Adapted from "Presentation to New England SOCAP," TARP Institute.

such rankings because these factors were out of their control. They needed to be ranked on items they influenced, like operator friendliness, helpfulness, and speed.

Figure 8-3 outlines various ways you can improve the quality and quantity of customer feedback and actively involve your entire staff in the process.

Remember, your employees deserve this information. The better informed they are, the better they will be able to serve your organization.

Figure 8-3.   **Suggestions for improving customer information.**

To gather more accurate customer data:

1. Call at least three customers a week—one happy, one unhappy, and one indifferent—to learn what each wants.

2. Call or meet at least three supervisors who deal directly with customers each week to find out how their week has gone.

3. Give everybody some experience dealing with customers: managers, data processors, accountants, and designers. This experience may be serving customers, visiting them, or seeing videotapes of them being served.

4. Invite customers in for a thorough look at your operation. "Debrief" them while they are there and listen to what's on their mind.

5. Get feedback from customers. Feedback includes both formal devices (comment cards, surveys) and informal talks directly with them.

6. Evaluate your last three new products or services. How many of them came from customers' ideas? How did these compare to new lines not inspired by customers?

7. Institute a specific system for learning and acting on customers' wants. Reward people for passing these ideas along. This includes salespeople, marketers, engineers, and servicepeople.

8. Reward managers, in part, on the basis of how in touch they and their people are with customers.

9. Share customer insights and feedback—good and bad—and post results where all employees can see them. Share the results of customer satisfaction ratings.

Reprinted by courtesy of Learning Dynamics, Inc.

Mail and Telephone Surveys

Mail and phone surveys are formal, yield hard data, and are usually best prepared and conducted by professionals. In designing these on your own, keep your mission statement in mind, specifically:

- What function are we trying to fulfill?
- Who are our customers now?
- Who would we like them to be?

When you've segmented your market, go after your customer base. Don't try to learn what everyone wants.

Focus Groups

Assemble a panel of customers, ex-customers, and noncustomers to find out what they think of your current and potential products and services.

Ask them in person the same questions you would use in your mail or telephone questionnaires and surveys.

A major telecommunications retailer conducted a formal customer satisfaction survey. The company's question was to the point: "What do you think of our customer service?" Two percent of the customers surveyed said excellent, 13 percent said good, 62 percent said they thought service was average, and the remaining 23 percent of the customers surveyed said that service was poor.[9]

Which conclusion would you agree with?

1. We're doing well; seventy-seven percent of our customers are satisfied.
2. We're doing pretty well; our average customer is satisfied.
3. We have a serious problem; twenty-three percent of our customers rate us as poor.

We would agree with item 3, first, because 23 percent is a high percentage of customers to be dissatisfied. If they are unhappy enough to look elsewhere or even to tell their friends about it, you are in trouble.

Second, because the 75 percent who rate you as good or average may not really be satisfied. Let's examine why.

Another question in the survey asked, "Would you return to us the next time you need telecommunications equipment?"

Although management considered "good" an acceptable rating, 30 percent of those who said service was good would not buy there again, as Figure 8-4 shows.

In conducting surveys, who asks, how they ask, and what they ask help determine your results. A large bank holding company's information service department surveyed its own internal customers, asking if they were satisfied with the service they got. When asked yes-no questions, or when asked to rate service on a scale of "very satisfied, satisfied," etc., the results looked pretty good. A company vice-president circulated a memo reporting that 90 percent were satisfied or better.

We know, however, that if customers don't give you the highest rating, something is probably wrong. Looking in more detail at the information service department's results, we found that only 35 percent of the responses indicated that customers were very satisfied; the rest were just satisfied.

Furthermore, the department itself selected the categories on which they wanted customers' ratings instead of asking customers what was important to them.

As part of a training project, Learning Dynamics surveyed the same customers—except that this survey asked open questions like "Tell me what services you currently use" and "Describe a typical interaction with

Figure 8-4. Rating vs. returns.

Satisfaction Rating	Would You Return? (percentage responding)	
	Yes	*No*
Excellent	98%	2%
Good	70	30
Fair	54	46

the company." There were several open questions about strengths and weaknesses. Only then were respondents asked to rate service. Finally they were asked for suggestions on improving service.

The results were dramatically different. Many customers had specific criticisms of the company's information service department and made comments like, "They're not even close to giving me what I want," "I have a tough time dealing with their policies and procedures—they seem to let things slide in the interest of cost reduction," and "They're defensive and rude; that's the policy."

Reducing their feelings to a number produced a rating of only 6.4 on a ten-point scale, far removed from the "90 percent satisfied or better" their own poll showed.

Lessons to learn from this discussion are these:

• You need to ask open questions to learn what people think is important.
• Sometimes customers are franker with an outsider than with their suppliers.

What all this means is that absolute measurements of satisfaction do not necessarily tell you how people really feel about you. You also need to learn just what "satisfaction" means to customers, what specific feeling of dissatisfaction will cause them to go elsewhere if they can. For example:

• A bank that had trained its tellers to make eye contact and greet customers found that this didn't make customers any happier. They learned that what really satisfied customers was completing their transactions in reasonable time.

• A major health insurer had tried to determine what was most important to its subscribers. It studied such factors as speed of answer, tone of response, and accuracy. They later found that what most complainers wanted was "clarity of explanation" and "reassurance that the problem would be resolved."

In these cases, what really mattered to customers was not what executives expected. As the researchers comment, "A number of key [satisfaction] dimensions are counterintuitive; therefore, management cannot and should not rely on its own intuition to select them." [10]

Let's take a closer look at this new customer information technology.

New Technology

There are four basic principles that drive research, using the new technology now available. They are (1) decision-focused, (2) coordinated, (3) multiple sources, and (4) standardized. [11]

Decision-Focused

The sole purpose of this sophisticated, professionally-conducted research is to provide data for making decisions. So you start by posing questions to which you want answers and end by studying conclusions and options.

For example, a health maintenance organization might start by asking, "What do our customers feel unhappiest about with our present level of service?" They might end with something like, "The complaints that we can do the most about are costs, delays, and uncaring personnel." In other words, improving these factors will give the company the biggest bang for their buck.

Coordinated

This kind of research does not exist in a departmental vaccuum. It looks at the service delivery system as a whole, from the customer's point of view. When you get results from the customer's viewpoint, you can coordinate all your service-delivery people: Marketing, sales, manufacturing, product/service research, and development all look at the results and ask how they can make things better for the customer. This leads to an ongoing information system to keep monitoring and updating data. You share this information with everybody, which, in turn, brings them closer together.

Multiple Sources

There are a number of techniques you can use and questions you can ask, but basically you want three kinds of information (opportunity, strategic, evaluation) from three sources (customers, noncustomers, and employees).

Opportunity

Opportunity data is information about future trends. The research will tell you about potential markets for your service and about customer needs that nobody is yet filling. For example, years ago, travelers told researchers they wanted an easy way to find "familiar service in an unfamiliar location." Holiday Inn came up with the answer of central booking, so travelers could call an 800 number and find the nearest Holiday Inn.[12]

Strategic

Next, your research gives you the information you need to decide what actions to take to achieve your goals.

For example, a bank asks its customers how satisfied they are. In looking at the results, bank executives notice that commercial customers are happier than retail customers. So for the next few months, the bank's strategy will be to concentrate its resources on its retail customers' concerns.

Evaluation

Third, the research helps you to evaluate your ongoing programs by providing information for assessing your performance. With this information, you can make decisions about monthly operations.

For example, an airport opened information booths to help travelers with problems or questions. Thinking these were not successful, management commissioned a formal market research project.

The researchers found that most of the passengers who had used the information booths were satisfied. But only 5 percent of passengers used them because the rest did not know where they were. Airport officials improved the visibility and advertising of the booths, so more passengers would be aware of them and use them.[13]

Sources for this information are:

- Customers, of course, because they are your best source of information
- Noncustomers, because they are potential customers and can give you a different perspective on things from your present customers
- Employees who are in constant touch with your customers and are an excellent source of information

Standardized

The last driving principle of this research is that you ask comparable questions of all three groups. So if you ask customers how satisfied they are with your service, you also need to ask noncustomers how satisfied they are with their current service and ask your employees how satisfied they think your customers are.

One utility asked customers what they considered most important in a service call. The repairperson's neatness was at the top of the list, because so many of them were leaving a mess in people's houses. But the repairpeople said they thought customers considered speed of completion most important.

Other Methods

Other kinds of high technology customer information systems include:

- *Conjoint analysis:* looking at how much of one feature (such as low price) customers will trade off to get something else (like better service)
- *Price sensitivity analysis:* determining how flexible price is for existing and potential services
- *Tracking studies:* measuring changes in customer attitudes, characteristics, and satisfaction
- *Environmental scanning:* identifying issues, problems, and opportunities in the marketplace

Good market research goes beyond mere head counting; it explains what the heads think and feel.

All of these methods can help you determine who your potential customers are, how they live, what they buy, and why they buy. From this information you can make key decisions about your customers.

A thought in closing: The U.S. Office of Consumer Affairs conducted exit surveys of 200 customers of a well-known Washington retailer.[14] They asked how satisfied customers were. The choices were *very satisfied, moderately satisfied, moderately dissatisfied,* and *very dissatisfied.*

Fifty-four percent of the respondents said they were very satisfied, by the way. But let's focus for a moment on the moderately satisfied category, not a bad rating. How many of the customers giving this response do you think had a specific complaint about something that happened in the store?

The answer is: All of them. And how many of the ninety-two customers who were less than very satisfied do you think complained to anyone in the store?

Zero. Not one of them said anything. And why not, do you suppose? When asked, they said because they expected mediocre service, because they didn't believe anything would be done if they had complained, and because the store's level of service was about the same as that of its competition.

In summary, if you're content to just retain market share, it may be good enough—at least until your competition offers better service. But if you have higher goals and are trying to increase your market, maintaining the status quo is not good enough. Because in many cases, the only way you can increase your market share is to take it away from your competition. So having your competition provide terrible service doesn't help you.

While providing better service is a matter of pride and an improved image, it also makes hard-nosed economic sense.

Notes

1. R. S. Lapp, "Star Quality the Lockheed Way," in Jay Sprechler, *When America Does It Right* (Norcross, Ga.: Industrial Engineering and Management Press, 1988), p. 19.
2. Tom Peters and Nancy Austin, *A Passion for Excellence* (New York: Random House, 1985).
3. *Ibid.*, p. 9.
4. *Ibid.*, p. 88.
5. Thomas J. Peters and Robert H. Waterman, Jr., *In Search of Excellence* (New York: Warner Books, 1982), p. 138.
6. "Florida Power & Light Company," American Productivity Center Case Study 39, 1984, p. 5.
7. Peters and Austin, *A Passion for Excellence*, p. 9.
8. Commtron, Annual Report, 1986.
9. John Goodman and Arlene Malech, "Issues in the Development of Valid, Actionable Satisfaction Measurement and Incentive Systems," TARP (Technical Assistance Research Programs Institute) working paper.
10. *Ibid.*
11. Information supplied by John Martin of Chadwick, Martin, Bailey Consultants, Boston.
12. W. Gerald Glover, R. Scott Morrison, Jr., and Alfred C. Briggs, Jr., "Making Quality Count," *The Cornell H.R.A. Quarterly*, May 1984.
13. Information supplied by John Martin of Chadwick, Martin, Bailey Consultants, Boston.
14. Goodman and Malech, "Issues in the Development of Valid, Actionable Satisfaction Measurement and Incentive Systems."

Nine

Step 4: Goals and Performance Measures

So far, you've evaluated what your organization is doing *internally* to drive or impede the customer-driven process. And you've begun the *external* focus on learning your customers' requirements. Now it is time for your next step in the strategy: translating the information you've gathered into goals and performance measurements.

Goals are not like New Year's resolutions. Rather, they are the focus for everyone in your organization. They say: "This is what we want to be in the future." We think the following is a good process:

1. Broad goals define the organization's purpose. This is called a mission statement.
2. Strategies (or general directional statements) say how goals will be achieved.
3. Objectives specify time-dependent milestones on the path to achieving goals.
4. Action plans spell out how you will allocate resources to meet the objectives. These include roles, responsibilities, and schedules.

In thinking about goal setting, the following test will guide you:

Goals Test

- Can people easily remember them? (Are there only a few?)
- Can people easily understand them? (Are they self-explanatory?)
- Is everyone's work linked to them? (Are they long-term and comprehensive?)
- Can you track progress toward achievement? (Are they measurable?)
- Are they visible? (Are they posted for all to see?)

Setting Goals

A useful first step in goal setting is to think of your ideal objectives. Answer the questions "Where do we want to be one year from now? . . . three years from now? How will we get there?"

Imagine an article written about your company and its service quality achievements in, say, *Fortune* magazine or *The Wall Street Journal*. Write a short summary of the article in Worksheet 16. Then answer the questions about what goals you'll need to set to live up to the story.

Suppose your internal evaluation showed the results in Worksheet 17. List the problems it shows in question 1.

What actions would these problems lead to? (List alternative actions in question 2.)

Once you've decided on strategy, you need to set objectives, time-dependent milestones on the path to achieving goals. In question 3, prioritize your list of alternative objectives. By ranking the importance of each alternative, you begin to define the road you will follow.

Some possible alternatives for action would be:

- Reassess your execution process, to improve your responsiveness to customers.
- Look for more building space.
- Evaluate hiring practices.
- Audit the results and the long-range impact of your service on your customers.

To rank these alternatives, answer:

- Do we have to do this before we can take some other action?
- Will this action impact on more than one part of the organization?
- How soon might this action produce a change that our customers will notice?

Although all four of the above alternatives can be undertaken simultaneously, the most immediate need is probably to change the method of handling inquiries, to stop alienating customers with an unfriendly approach. Next would be to seek more space. Next you might evaluate hiring policies, and, finally, audit the results and long-term impact of your services.

Make Goals Visible

Whether you call them goals, objectives, or targets, it is crucial that you make your desired outcomes visible. This way, they declare your purpose

(text continues on page 112)

Worksheet 16. Imagining the Future

To determine your ideal goal and to sharpen your vision for the future, complete the following:

1. Describe a *Fortune* magazine or *The Wall Street Journal* article written about your company and its customer service quality achievements one year from now.

_____

_____

_____

_____

_____

_____

_____

_____

2. Read what you have just written and then answer the following questions to help formulate your goals:
   a. What clues has my description given me about long-term goals?

   _____

   _____

   _____

   b. How realistic are these goals, given our present resources?

   _____

   _____

   _____

   c. What are the key steps required to achieve these long-term goals?

   _____

   _____

   _____

Reprinted by courtesy of Learning Dynamics, Inc.

Worksheet 17. Case Study: Your Internal Evaluation

Your organization's internal evaluation showed the following results:

Content: We're doing the right things.

Execution: We may not be doing them the right way. For example, our CSRs have to ask for a customer's number first so that they can look it up on the computer before they listen to what the customer has to say. Customers complain about this. Maybe we should emphasize listening to the customer and building rapport before we demand their number.

Structure: Our facilities are barely adequate now; we will have to expand in the next year. Our organizational setup is in good shape. Our hiring process is spotty.

Outcome: We don't really know our results because we don't measure on an ongoing basis.

Impact: We have no idea what our impact is on customers or employees.

Exercise

1. List the top problems discovered in this evaluation.

_____

_____

_____

2. What alternatives for action would this lead to?

_____

_____

_____

3. Prioritize your alternative actions by answering these questions:
   a. Do I have to do this before I can take some other action?
   b. Will this action impact on more than one part of the organization? How?
   c. How soon will this action produce a change that our customers will notice?

_____

_____

_____

Reprinted by courtesy of Learning Dynamics, Inc.

in life and your commitment to your future. At the same time, you let everyone know both the goals and your progress toward reaching them. This is critically important to building team spirit.

The quality credo of National Westminster Bank is an outstanding example:

> National Westminster USA will develop and deliver products and services that conform to customers' financial and information requirements. Our goal is to be recognized as the premier quality bank in each of the markets we serve.
>
> * * *
>
> All marketing, products, processes, systems and training will be designed to prevent errors and to provide customers with consistently high levels of quality, which we will continuously monitor.
>
> * * *
>
> If errors or service problems do occur, emphasis will be placed on timely and courteous resolution, including appropriate communication with the customer.
>
> * * *
>
> Success will be measured in terms of our ability to meet customer requirements, and employees will be rewarded for quality performance.

The credo spells out the behaviors the bank wants in this section on customers:

> The everyday things we do to better serve customers are obvious, but they bear repeating. These actions apply to everyone because, even where there is no direct customer contact, everything we do is related to serving customers:
>
> - We listen to our customers to determine their needs and then attempt to fill those needs.
> - We respond in a thoughtful, professional and timely manner.
> - We deliver our products and services error free and in a consistent manner.
> - We price our products and services fairly.
> - We are always respectful and courteous.
> - We do our work in essential staff areas as cost effectively as possible, because we invest our principal resources in customer-driven activities.

So publicize your goals companywide. Make certain everyone in the organization is aware of them and knows you will reward their achievements.

Measuring Performance

The question often arises: Is it possible to measure service performance? After all, in a manufacturing environment, you can test, inspect, count scrap, and analyze rejects to determine causes of failures, but such measures are difficult to apply to an intangible service. However, as we've said, we think you can measure service quality by examining content, process, structure, outcome, and impact. You can take this process a step further in the way you establish service quality requirements.

But first, let's examine what quality is. *Quality* has several meanings, including *features, characteristics, good* and *excellence*. But *quality service* has only one meaning: "The ability to meet customers' requirements."

Services don't have "high" quality or "low" quality: They either meet customers' requirements or they don't. A French restaurant has no "higher" quality than a McDonald's, because their customers have different needs. The French restaurant's diners want gourmet food and elegant service; McDonald's customers want predictably good food, at low prices, in a hurry. Indeed, French restaurants that have opened for lunch near factories have been disappointed because their clientele is looking for speed, not a dining experience.

Establishing Service Quality Requirements

The more you can specify requirements, the better you will serve customers. Granted, human beings are messy; they don't "herd" well and they don't fit into boxes. But unless you know what requirements to meet, you can only guess at what people want.

To put this into perspective, let's compare product requirements, which focus on systems and tasks, to service requirements, which focus on people,[1] as shown in Figure 9-1.

With products, you start by defining the customer's needs—the specific quality characteristics that will satisfy customers (usually designed by the engineers). With quality service, you also start by determining what customers want, but you don't ask engineers, you ask your customers what "quality service" means to them.

In manufacturing (a continuing process) the next step is to determine carefully requirements for the end product: drawings, raw-product specs, and machinery requirements, for example. Quality is then defined as "conformance to these requirements."

In service (not a continuous process), *set specifications* means focus on customer requirements. These are designed into the service delivery system, which is service's equivalent of a production line; procedures, policies, and decisions are your "machinery." You also document procedures, measure efficiency, plan layout, and select equipment.

Figure 9-1. Product vs. service requirements.

Products	Service
Focus:	Focus:
Correct and prevent defects.	Improve customer (internal and external) relationships for 100 percent satisfaction.
Design Quality:	Design Quality:
Define customer needs.	Determine customer requirements.
	Share clear goals for superior quality/ service.
Set Standards:	Set Specifications:
Design the product to be defect-free.	Do right things right.
	Design system to meet customer requirements.
	Motivate and empower employees.
Check Conformance:	Measure Performance:
Output.	Input.
Process.	Process.
	Output.

Reprinted by courtesy of Learning Dynamics, Inc.

Next in manufacturing, you check conformance to requirements: You inspect and test the final product (output) and monitor the production process to see if it performs as it is supposed to (process).

In service, the next step is to measure performance. Remember, all work consists of taking input, processing it, and producing output. While products just measure outputs and process, service also measures inputs.

The input measurements are crucial to meeting specifications; they are more than the tasks, procedures, and systems needed to meet specifications and doing right things right. The "biggie" here is your employees and what they are, or are not, bringing to the customer. As we mentioned earlier, people can't be put into boxes, and you don't want to stifle creativity and innovation. Nevertheless, you have to know how well your employees' esteem needs are being met; their levels of satisfaction and dissatisfaction in key areas; and what they are saying and feeling about the organization, the boss, the system, customers, and you. All of these factors have a direct, immediate, and powerful impact on how customers are treated. You can measure these factors through employee attitude surveys and other service audits.

The process is how you treat customers. (A bank may meet customers' output needs by cashing checks accurately, but if tellers are rude, it's failing on process.) You can measure process by studying operating, financial, and cost-of-service data; conducting internal audits; and observing transactions. Some companies monitor telephone calls and use "secret shoppers."

The output in service is whether you've met your customers' needs, internal as well as external. You measure customer satisfaction by such indirect methods as tracking customer complaints, soliciting and evaluating feedback, measuring market share, identifying internal problems, and other internal feedback methods.

Specifications and Key Indicators

To measure goals, you need to state them as behaviors or in quantitative and/or qualitative measures. What, for example, will achieving your goal look like? How will you know when you've achieved it? What new behaviors will you see? What baseline measures will show you that you are doing the right things right? Will it be market share, amount of repeat business, trend of customer complaints?[2]

If your goal is to have contact people be more helpful and deliver quality service, one way to state this goal is: "Contact people will identify themselves by name, use the customer's name (if they know it), and determine the nature of the problem before asking for details."

For example, an airline determined that its target market, business travelers, wanted first and foremost to have their flight arrive on time. They also liked being checked in promptly and cheerfully. The airline might set specifications like:

- Have every flight arrive within ten minutes of schedule.
- Don't make passengers wait more than five minutes to check in.
- Make eye contact at least once during the transaction.
- Address passengers by name when known.

Some key indicators for measuring success in achieving these goals would be:

- The number of people waiting on line
- The number of times flights arrive more than ten minutes later than scheduled

For another example, a stockbroker may learn that a new investor wants "a good return with maximum safety." How could this requirement be translated into specifications?

The broker might suggest top corporate bonds, government bonds only, or utility stocks. The key indicators could be AAA rating for corporate bonds or interest rate of at least 6 percent.

We suggest you now try Worksheet 18, on setting measurable goals. First, complete your statement: What specifications and actions are required to fulfill your goal? That is content (right things), execution (right things right), and structure (resources and facilities). Then, what key indicators—measurable behaviors or data—will prove that you are achieving your goal? These are outcomes and impact.

Dimensions of Service Quality

According to one group of researchers, customer expectations about service can be broken down into the ten categories shown in Worksheet 19.

But sometimes customers' requirements are vague, so you need to supply the specific measures. For example, customers might identify "friendliness" as one of their requirements for your service people. To get behavioral equivalents for "friendliness," try to get examples. Ask customers, "Can you describe a time when a contact person was very friendly?" Or look for specifics by asking, "How would you want a 'friendly' employee to behave?"

The same is true for internal customers. A report- and presentation-writing department found its customers desired "concise" and "professional" reports. The supplier showed customers different samples and asked for definitions of these terms. They learned "concise" meant "no more than five pages and four charts," and "professional" meant "embossed covers" and "right-justified printing."

Customers don't always say what they require. A hotel may find in interviews that potential guests stress quiet and good food. They won't mention clean rooms and competent front-desk help. In service language, cleanliness and good help are "minimum requirements to compete": Customers assume every hotel has them and won't patronize you otherwise. They will mention extras or what we call "value added." (See Figure 9-2 for an example of a hotel that defines, measures, and rewards service.)

And customers don't always know what they want or need. For example, for years people grumbled about the lack of quick package delivery. Few people told consumer researchers that they wanted an inexpensive, overnight delivery service because they never thought of it.

Worksheet 18. Performance Measurement

Goals need to be measurable—so state them in behavioral terms, i.e., in quantifiable and/or qualifiable measures.

This means behaviors you can see or real measures like time, size, dollars, numbers, percentages. What, for example, will achieving your goal look like? How will you know when you've achieved it? What new behaviors will you see? What baseline measures will show you that you are doing the right thing right?

Your goal is to "deliver 100 percent customer satisfaction with excellent service." How would you state the goal in behavioral terms you can measure?

1. Specifications of actions required to fulfill goal:

_____

_____

_____

_____

2. Key indicators to prove goal achievement:

_____

_____

_____

Reprinted by courtesy of Learning Dynamics, Inc.

But Federal Express (and later others) were imaginative enough to see this as a potentially profitable business.[3]

Performance Problems

When the measurement system indicates that you aren't meeting customers' requirements, you need to do something to correct the situation. The basic approach is to identify and remedy the problem on as low a level as possible.

If an individual employee isn't meeting standards, that employee and his or her supervisor can decide how to improve. Most performance problems stem from lack of knowledge, lack of motivation, or environmental hindrances, and, with training, your supervisors will be able to identify the cause.

Worksheet 19. Dimensions of Service Quality

Here are the ten quality dimensions. Rate yourself from your customer's perspective by checking the appropriate box to the right.

Dimension	Examples of Evaluative Criteria	Excellent	Adequate	Needs Improvement	Serious Problem
Tangibles	Appearance of physical facilities and personnel	☐	☐	☐	☐
Reliability	Consistency of performance and dependability	☐	☐	☐	☐
Responsiveness	Willingness and ability to provide prompt service	☐	☐	☐	☐
Communication	Explaining service to customers in language they can understand	☐	☐	☐	☐
Credibility	Trustworthiness of customer-contact personnel	☐	☐	☐	☐
Security	Confidentiality of transactions	☐	☐	☐	☐
Competence	Knowledge and skill of customer-contact personnel	☐	☐	☐	☐
Courtesy	Friendliness of customer-contact personnel	☐	☐	☐	☐
Understanding/ Knowing customers	Making an effort to ascertain a customer's specific requirements	☐	☐	☐	☐
Accessibility	Ease of contacting service firm by telephone	☐	☐	☐	☐

If an individual customer isn't having his or her needs met, grant employees enough authority to fix the situation on the spot. For example, if a copier serviceperson hasn't finished repairs by quitting time, he or she should be able to work overtime to get it done.

If large numbers of customers aren't having their needs met, the first line of defense is customer-contact people. Individually or in groups, they can probably tell you where the system is falling down and what you need to do to remedy it.

Let's look at an economic analysis of why contact people are so important. There are three basic people who can catch a mistake:

(text continues on page 120)

Figure 9-2. Marriott's Camelback Inn.

From the moment you arrive at this lovely Scottsdale, Arizona, resort, you sense something special. It's not just the beauty of the place; there are many beautiful resorts. It is the people.

   . . . The valet parking attendant seems genuinely pleased to see you.
   . . . The front desk check-in is flawless and extremely friendly.
   . . . The bell station personnel are at the ready; filled with information to inform and entertain while driving you to your room (where a complimentary wine, cheese, and fruit basket awaits you).

There are special touches everywhere you turn . . . all sending a message "We're glad you're here. How can we make your stay even more enjoyable?" For example: no smoking rooms easily available; identifying signs on the plants, in and out of doors; a huge basket of apples in the lobby; streets and grounds being swept and maintained as carefully as the beautiful sitting room/lobby.

Dining, however, was a mixed blessing when we were last there; wonderful food; many in help; but alas, disorganized, slow service. Going to prove that service excellence is not an easy task even in the best organizations. (They have recognized the problem and since installed a new dining management team.)

A long interview with Wynn Tyner, manager of this remarkable resort, reveals the "secret" of its success: Guest satisfaction drives the system, its management, and staff. Whatever guests ask, the answer is "Yes, tell me what you'd like me to do."

Everybody's Job Is Important

There are 800 employees and sixty managers (promoted from within) at Camelback. All are focused on guest satisfaction through a property-wide award campaign called GS1—Guest Service 1st. Many wear GS1 badges with fresh blue ribbons, which announce their participation in the campaign. All will gladly explain the GS1 goals.

Wynn Tyner explains the evaluation system: pre-set measurable goals, ranked against all other Marriotts and Marriott Resorts in a thirteen-period cycle. (Camelback was second overall and first in resorts when we visited. However, in a later conversation we learned they had won the overall #1.)

There are a variety of rewards: Certificates of Appreciation, cash incentives, Golden Camels, Gold Key Awards, and special awards for achieving "Stretch Goals."

But there is more to it than the Marriott's system of goals, measures, and rewards. It is the obvious commitment and behavior modeling of Wynn Tyner. He walks what he talks, and his sincerity gains the buy-in of his people. How else can you explain hairdresser Dennis Winters, exuding enthusiasm, boasting of being #1 GS1 . . . and coming in on a rare day-off Saturday? Now that's customer satisfaction!

Wynn, asked how he has learned all of this, when he looks about nineteen years old and works in such a remote location, replies, "It's just common sense. It's a lot easier and more fun managing a hotel filled with happy guests than with unhappy, complaining guests."

Our experience is that "common sense ain't so common." And that, however he learned it, Wynn Tyner is the epitome of a customer-driven manager. Or, as he describes his job—"The Customer's General Manager."

1. The originator. This could be, for instance, a data processor who enters the wrong price in your cash register system, looks at the printout, and corrects it.
2. The customer-contact person. This could perhaps be the cashier who enters the item code, notices the price is wrong, and calls up the data processing department to have them correct it.
3. The customer. He or she takes the item home, notices that the price on the bill doesn't match the posted price, and calls the store for a correction.

Evaluating People

The key difference between service and manufacturing is people.

Human performance is critically affected by how people feel—especially if they are satisfied or dissatisfied by their job, treatment, boss, company policies, and other issues. If an auto assembly line worker hates carburetors, he can still do a good job. But if an automobile service writer hates cars, he's probably not going to serve customers well.

In addition, humans can choose how they'll meet customer requirements, which is what you want. You might specify, "Greet every customer," but you do not tell people how to greet them. ("Have a good day!") Some individuals may say, "Good evening," and others "Hi, y'all," depending on the circumstances.[4]

What you don't need is a system that encourages conformity and discourages creative thinking, innovation, and problem-solving. You can't control or supervise each interaction with customers in any case, so add "meet employee esteem needs" to your quality improvement plan.

Our Evaluation System is set out in Figure 9-3.

Measuring Service: Some Examples

Here is how some outstanding companies measure service.

American Express notes that everyone in the service industry knows the most difficult thing to measure is how a customer feels. Its approach is to survey how customers feel about a single transaction in relation to their future use of the card, what they'll tell their friends, etc. They feel "this transforms an area of so-called soft information into a documented measurement tool."[5]

AT&T also tries to "focus aggressively on those service and administrative areas traditionally thought of as being in the 'soft' area of customer needs and expectations." It has developed a set of guidelines to help employees concentrate on delivering what customers need.[6]

Figure 9-3. Evaluating human performance.

Input	Specifications	Key Indicators
Level of skill/training	Hiring process	Turnover
Satisfaction/dissatisfaction level	Career track	Attitude survey
Reward system	Behavior being rewarded	Other costs
Motivation/dedication	Problems reported	Lost customers
Enablement/empowerment	What people say	Lost orders

TRW has defined some of the standards that customer and servicer need to agree on in computer repair:

- Response time
- Repair time
- System availability (uptime)
- How to call the service company
- How to speak to the customer
- Emergency repairs
- Preventive maintenance
- How to report service activities to the customer
- How often to review performance with the customer
- Dealing with problems
- Customer responsibilities

Agreement with each customer lets you know what to measure, says TRW.[7]

Caterpillar has a formula to measure how frequently each maintenance activity on its machines has to be performed, and how difficult it is.[8]

Metropolitan Life Insurance Company found insurance customers had five concerns: reliability (notices sent on schedule and correctly), responsiveness (processing all claims within five days), tangibles (convenient offices with modern equipment), assurance (that personal data will be kept confidential), and empathy (understandable correspondence and conversations, free of jargon).

From this definition, Met Life was able to develop an instrument that could quantify service performance (as the difference between customer's expectations and the company's performance).

Met Life found that no company meets all customers' expectations; "the better companies merely had a smaller gap."[9]

Winnebago distributes such parts data as same-day and next-day fill rates; back-ordered inventory; comparisons of order points to projections; items picked, packed, and shipped per employee; and sales per employee and dealer.[10]

Citicorp is clear on the two kinds of things to be measured: conformance to objective internal standards, including accuracy, responsiveness, and timeliness; and subjective satisfaction of external customers, measured by the number who say they are pleased. "While productivity measures may reflect only intermediate steps in the multistep chain of service delivery, true service indicators measure the entire experience from the customer's perspective," it believes.[11]

Statistics are okay, but Anheuser-Busch believes you need the human element too. So it has "flavor panels" meet daily at each of the company's eleven breweries to judge the aroma, appearance, and taste of beer.[12]

Writing Goal Statements

When you've established customer requirements, your next step is to write goal statements to meet them. An important principle in goal achievement is not to try to do too much at once. If you set your initial goals too high, you may get discouraged and give up. That's why we recommend the "Swiss cheese" approach.

"Swiss cheesing" a problem means poking holes in it to break it up into smaller problems. In this case, you break your long-term goal into smaller goals. By achieving interim goals, you'll get more of a feeling of accomplishment when you reach benchmarks of progress.

For example, if you provide preventive maintenance to computers and you want to reduce downtime from 5 percent to less than 1 percent, you might establish interim goals such as 4 percent after one month, 3 percent after two, and 1 percent after three.

If you didn't set these benchmarks, at the end of the first month you might say, "Well, we've reduced downtime a little, but we still have a long way to go."

It's important to communicate this performance standard in writing to employees all down the line.

For example, Met Life found that 80 percent of policies were issued within three days of approval, 90 percent within four days, and 100 percent within five. So they set their goal at 5 percent higher (85 percent within three days and 95 percent within four).[13]

There are several benefits to telling employees exactly what you expect:

1. Such documentation helps you see how each procedure fits into your service strategy as a whole.

2. It lets everybody know who is responsible for what tasks.
3. It reduces conflicts and misunderstandings on who is going to do what.
4. Having it in writing helps new employees learn the job.
5. It helps pinpoint problems and areas for improvement.
6. It may help you with government agencies and lawsuits.

When you've communicated what you want your people to do, check to see they do it and that they are producing the results you want.

You can also use traditional methods of measuring performance, such as observations by supervisors, inspection of the physical plant, interviewing contact people, and analyzing financial data.

The most important quality measure is what your customers think, since the definition of quality is "meeting customers' requirements." Your customer research will tell you this. Your goals will also tell you how to measure performance in each functional area, whether it's size of customer base, percentage of repeat business, market share, profits, or other baseline measures.

And you can come up with your own ways of measuring performance, as executives at the Boca Raton Hotel did. They call theirs a Cost of Error Analysis.[14]

They identified two types of errors:

1. *Those you can measure.* For example, if someone breaks a plate, the cost is easy to calculate. At Boca Raton, broken plates were costing the hotel $200,000 a year. Hotel management was able to reduce this through staff training. Another example: Unused cream and butter are supposed to go back to the pantry. If they are allowed to spoil, there is a definite cost attached, which people can be trained to reduce.

2. *Those errors you can't put a pricetag on but which affect guests' perceptions of quality, such as rooms not being clean.* Most of these errors stem from poor communication. For example, one of the hotel's meeting rooms was booked for two meetings at the same time. Clearly this type of error is damaging to the hotel. In this case, the sales and convention departments had each booked the room; to prevent a recurrence, the hotel instituted procedures to make sure the departments communicate better.

Another example: The hotel owns a boat that was booked to launch a cruise at 5:30 P.M., with dinner at 6:30 P.M. The hotel's kitchen was told only about the dinner and delivered the food promptly at 6:30, never having been informed that the cruise started an hour earlier.

Now try the following exercise on performance measurement. Read the case study in Worksheet 20 and come up with a way to measure performance.[15]

Worksheet 20. Case Study: Performance Measurement

The California seafood restaurant chain the Rusty Pelican has decided to start measuring its performance. What measures would you suggest?

_____

_____

_____

_____

_____

_____

_____

Reprinted by courtesy of Learning Dynamics, Inc.

Worksheet 21. Performance Goals

Rusty Pelican's goal was "attentive service." What are some behaviors that would mean "attentive service?"

_____

_____

_____

_____

_____

_____

Reprinted by courtesy of Learning Dynamics, Inc.

How did you do? Difficult? It is hard to write performance measures without goals.

Now look at the performance goals for the restaurant in Worksheet 21. Then write your performance measures with goals in mind.

You'll find a sample of the Rusty Pelican performance measures in Figure 9-4.

In summary, without a clear vision of where you are going and without specific behaviors to measure, it is almost impossible to achieve any goal. Goal setting, strategies, objectives, and action plans are an ongoing,

Figure 9-4. Rusty Pelican performance measures.

The Rusty Pelican restaurants developed the following as criteria for assessing attentive service:

- Server speaks to customer within two minutes of seating.
- Beverage service at table within four minutes of order.
- Check for reorder of cocktail and customer satisfaction within five minutes of delivery of first cocktail.
- Customers asked whether they care to order within four minutes after beverage service (or if no beverage ordered, within four minutes of seating).
- Appetizers, salad, or wine delivered within five minutes.
- Entrée served within sixteen minutes of order.
- Dessert, coffee, and after-dinner drinks served within five minutes after plates cleared.
- Check presented within four minutes after dessert (or after plates cleared, if no dessert).
- Cash or credit cards picked up within two minutes of being placed by customer on table.

---

ever-changing part of this process, and one that we think will be a way of life for successful enterprises from now on.

Notes

1. Carol A. King, "Service-Oriented Quality Control," *The Cornell H.R.A. Quarterly,* November 1984.
2. John F. Rockart, "Chief Executives Define Their Own Data Needs," *Harvard Business Review,* March–April 1979.
3. Leonard Berry, Valarie A. Zeithaml, and A. Parasuraman, "Quality Counts in Services, Too," *Business Horizons,* May–June 1985.
4. King, "Service-Oriented Quality Control."
5. MaryAnne Rasmussen, "Service Quality: Our Most Strategic Weapon," in Jay Sprechler, *When America Does It Right* (Norcross, Ga.: Industrial Engineering and Management Press, 1988), p. 112.
6. Roberta J. Coleman, "AT&T: Building on a Quality Tradition to Ensure Quality Service Delivery," in Sprechler, *When America Does It Right,* p. 128.
7. Jack Smith, "Quality in Computer Services," in Sprechler, *When America Does It Right,* p. 138.
8. James E. Redpath, Jr., "Delivering Quality Service to the Caterpillar Earthmoving Customer," in Sprechler, *When America Does It Right,* p. 198.
9. John J. Falzon, "Met Life's Quest for Quality," in Sprechler, *When America Does It Right,* p. 222.

10. Robert W. Post and Randal L. Fingarson, "Quality Service Program," in Sprechler, *When America Does It Right,* p. 297.
11. Dinah Nemeroff, "Quality Consumer Financial Services," in Sprechler, *When America Does It Right,* p. 76.
12. William L. Rammes, "Making Friends Is Our Business," in Sprechler, *When America Does It Right,* p. 31.
13. Falzon, in Sprechler, *When America Does It Right,* p. 219.
14. W. Gerald Glover, R. Scott Morrison, Jr., and Alfred C. Briggs, "Making Quality Count," *The Cornell H.R.A. Quarterly,* May 1984.
15. D. Daryl Wyckoff, "New Tools for Achieving Service Quality," *The Cornell H.R.A. Quarterly,* November 1984.

Ten

Step 5: Customer-Driven Management

Once your customer information research is in place and your goals and measures are set, your next step is to establish a customer-driven culture. This is a big task, but not an overwhelming one. It requires—in addition to your personal leadership—new strategies and systems to drive behavior and to guide everyone in how to deliver service quality in your new customer-friendly culture.

We call the process "customer-driven management."

As we've said, the U.S. economy is dominated by companies that perform rather than produce. As a result, customers who once focused on quality of product now focus on quality of service, so much so that customer-driven service quality has become the new fast track of the American economy.

Recall that companies rated above-average in service grow twice as fast, charge about 10 percent more, and make 1,100 percent more in return on sales!

In short, our culture has changed from:

Old Commitments	New Commitments
Productivity	Meeting customer
Technology	requirements
Cost-cutting	

Creating Customer-Driven Strategies

Your strategy, in the customer-driven management context, is your distinctive and unique method of providing service quality that sets you apart from your competition.

To get a look at your strategy, begin by flowcharting your service cycle from your customer's point of view. Think about where your service starts and ends and what a customer has to do to receive your product or service. For example, with a delivery service, your cycle doesn't start with the package pickup but when the customer first learns about your company (sees your ad in the Yellow Pages, for example). And it doesn't end when the package is received but when the customer (sender) learns that the other person has received it.

Consider the input everyone involved has to provide. (For the delivery service, input includes telephone answering, order write-up, dispatch, and pick-up.) Next consider what choices people in the system make and what major options they have. For the delivery service that might include whether the package is more or less than two pounds; if it's more, there's an extra charge.

Once you've thought your process through and listed each point in your service cycle, you're ready to flowchart it. First, fill in how things are supposed to go, and second, what can go wrong that might cost you customers. A hospital's cycle would look like Figure 10-1.

Think about the process your customers go through in dealing with your organization and what can go wrong. Then do a flowchart in Worksheet 22 of the cycle of service from initial contact to completed purchase or receipt of your service.

Customer-Centered Systems

Systems, including policies, procedures, methods, technologies, means of communication, and processes, are all elements that drive the behavior of your people. Most of today's business systems have been designed to meet organizational needs, not customer needs. So you may need to redesign your systems to support your customer-driven strategy.

The Walt Disney Company is an outstanding example of effective delivery: it brings people into its system early. Every employee has to attend Disney University and pass a "Traditions I" course before going on to specialized training. Traditions I is an all-day experience where the new hire learns Disney philosophy and operating methods. No one, from vice president to entry-level part-timers, is exempt from the course.

At Disney theme parks, the systems support for people "on stage" is dramatic. For example, there are hundreds of phones hidden in the bushes, hotlines to a central question-answering service. And the amount of effort put into the daily cleanup amazes even the most calloused outside observers. In these and scores of other ways, overkill marks every aspect of Disney's strategic approach to its customers.[1]

Figure 10-1. The service cycle.

Here is an example of a service cycle for a hospital emergency room. The inner boxes represent how things are supposed to go. The outer boxes are things that can go wrong.

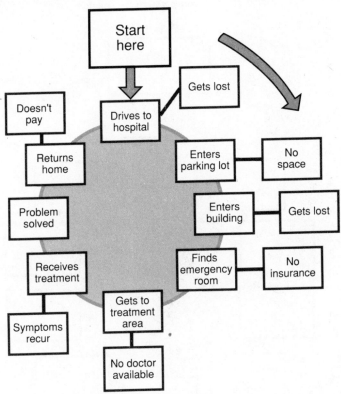

Reprinted by courtesy of Learning Dynamics, Inc.

Improving the Service System

To evaluate your systems, look at things from the customer's point of view. You just did this in the cycle of service flowchart, which gives you a blueprint of the steps in service delivery. It separates what customers can see from what they can't and pinpoints places where things can go wrong. Let's take as an example opening an account with a stockbroker. What are the steps involved?[2] Look at Figure 10-2.

(text continues on page 131)

Worksheet 22. The Service Cycle Flowchart

Fill in the flowchart below with the service cycle for your company's customers. Note (1) what customers go through to receive your service and (2) where problems in the cycle might occur that could cause you to lose customers.

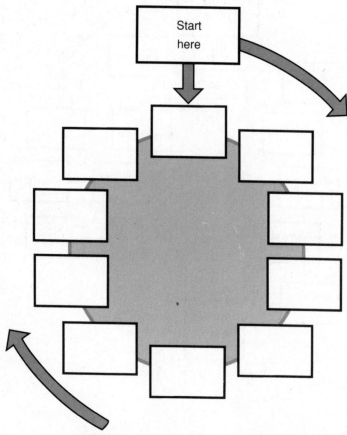

Reprinted by courtesy of Learning Dynamics, Inc.

Figure 10-2. The stockbroker system.

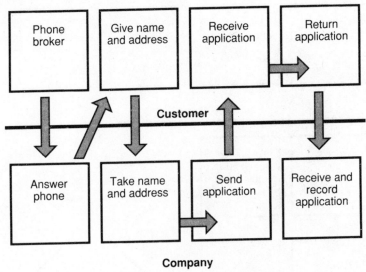

Reprinted by courtesy of Learning Dynamics, Inc.

Now what are some of the steps the customer does not see in receiving and recording the application? (See Figure 10-3.) Possibilities include:

- Checking that all information is included
- Calling or writing the customer if something is missing
- Getting credit approval for a margin account
- Entering the information correctly

The hallmark of an excellent service system is integrating the seen and unseen processes to support the service strategy.

Charting the process shows where the system might go awry. When you isolate these "fail points," you can focus on preventing them. For example, in the brokerage firm, CSRs' answers to customer questions proved crucial, so management scripted answers to the most common questions. The firm also trained CSRs in communication techniques, staffed the center so phones never went unanswered, and recorded all transactions to ensure accuracy. The revised process is in Figure 10-4.

Looking at the process as a whole helps you establish time guidelines, which can affect profitability. The brokerage set an initial guideline of thirty minutes to open an account. As they gained more experience, they adjusted the standard.

Figure 10-3. The stockbroker system invisible to customers.

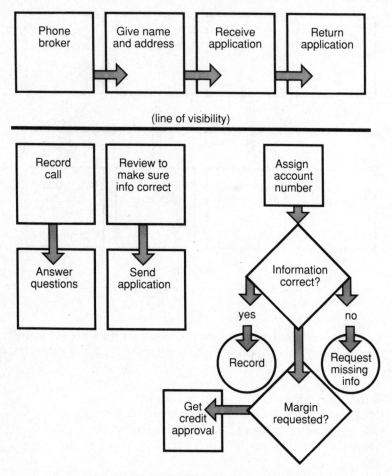

Reprinted by courtesy of Learning Dynamics, Inc.

Flowcharting also helps you measure costs. Since you know how long each step should take, you can attach costs to the various parts of the process.

It also lets you measure competitive differences. If you see your competitors are outdoing you in one service aspect, you can isolate the disadvantage and modify your design.

Finally, the flowchart helps you integrate new elements. When you offer a new service, you can see how it fits in with existing ones.

Figure 10-4. The revised stockbroker system.

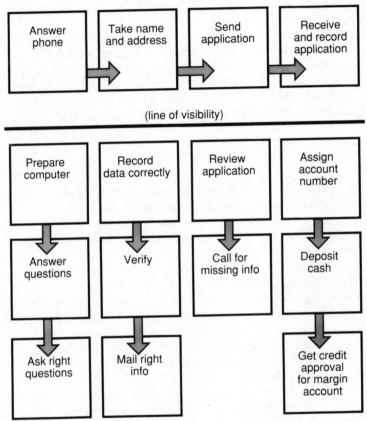

Reprinted by courtesy of Learning Dynamics, Inc.

Smoothing Demand

Customers all seem to arrive at the same time, such as lunch hour, weekends, or Christmas vacation, depending on your industry. You want to be able to meet these peak demands. But since you can't inventory service, any time you spend waiting for customers is lost forever.

The best way out of this dilemma is to smooth customer demand,[3] which requires customer cooperation. One way to accomplish this is to offer appointments and reservations. For example, suppose a dealer of imported cars wants to build its repair business. If the policy is "first come–first served," many customers will try to bring their car in early, creating chaos, delays, and bad feelings. But if the dealer offers appointments, the work will be smooth and people happier in knowing when their car will be ready.

Price incentives are another way to shift demand to off-peak hours. The phone company does this with lower night and weekend rates.

With government, "customers" "pay" with their time. The public learns that coming at popular hours (early morning, lunch, late afternoon) results in longer waits. As a result, anyone who possibly can comes at off-peak hours (like mid-morning and mid-afternoon).

Improving Technology

Technological improvements include systems such as electronic funds transfers and hardware such as automatic teller machines (ATMs).

There are so many ways to use new technology that a whole book could be devoted to the subject. So let's look at just one innovation: the ATM.

An ATM handles transactions for 60 percent less money than a human teller. Although banks have spent over a billion dollars on ATMs, not all depositors like them. And it's not for lack of effort; banks have tried almost everything, such as drawings for trips, color TVs, and money donated to children's cancer research, to get customers to use ATMs.

And they've tried the stick along with the carrot by forcing customers to use their ATM card to talk to a live teller!

Why aren't ATMs wildly successful?

A technological innovation like an ATM works only if customers want it, since they participate directly in the service process. If they don't want it, you'll have a hard time making them accept it. In the ATM case, a great many people want personal contact more than just convenience and fast service. Again we say, stay in touch with your customers' requirements.

Satisfying the Customer

If your system does not meet the acid test of customer satisfaction, you'll need to change the system, the process, or some other input in your cycle of service.

To illustrate the impact of systems and policies on customers, let's review your answers to an earlier exercise. Turn back to Worksheet 4, "Report to the Boss." Knowing what you know now, how do you feel about your responses?

These problems are generally caused by systems that put organizational convenience ahead of customer needs. If the organization's goal was to meet customer needs, it would establish customer-friendly policies and systems.

Suggested Answers to Worksheet 4

1. If it doesn't cost any extra to change sizes and the $10 charge causes disgruntlement, eliminate the charge. Even if it does cost extra, $10 is not worth angering customers.

2. The problem with saying "unreasonable customers are not worth having" is: How do you define "unreasonable"? Often this definition gets wider and wider until anyone who inconveniences you is "unreasonable." Instead of "offering all solutions available," just ask the customer what he or she wants, then listen and work something out. And obviously, don't tell them you can produce something when you cannot.

3. Educate customers so they know what to expect. Remind them in advance that they are getting photocopies, not "printed" ones.

4. When customers call for a quote, repeat their specifications to them. Ask a few questions about borders and so on. Perhaps you could mail or fax written confirmations of phone quotes to resolve disputes before the order is billed.

5. Reexamine strategy. To be the fastest in the industry, find a way to cut the turnaround time. If customers want rush orders, provide them, and charge appropriately.

6. Protecting dealers is praiseworthy. The only problem we can see here is that perhaps the definition of dealer is too narrow. Large orders deserve a discount, even if they are not in the trade and not offering the product for resale.

7. This is the height of insensitivity to customers. If people want to order on the 800 line, don't tell them they can't. Get more lines, if necessary, and increase prices a few cents to cover the cost of the 800 number.

8. Presidents and managers don't need protection; they need to talk more to customers, particularly upset ones. This policy does not undercut CSRs. Talking to customers is the best way to learn what is happening in the marketplace.

The Three Faces of Customer-Driven Management

To survive and grow, every organization needs all of its managers to take on three roles:

1. *Customer-Champion.* Learning what customers want and making certain they get it.

- Acting as the eyes, ears, and voice of the customer in your organization.
- Meeting personally with customers to find out what's on their mind.
- Proactively "thinking customer" to meet their requirements.

2. *Coach-Counselor.* Empowering subordinates to deliver customer-driven service.

- Giving subordinates responsibility for meeting customers' requirements.
- Meeting employees' needs for knowledge and resources, so they can be accountable.
- Motivating and rewarding.

3. *Integrator.* Building an internal network to meet customer requirements.

- Working with different departments, levels, and functions to integrate and measure process and performance.
- Building a customer-focused team—boss, peers, and subordinates.
- Providing motivation, implementation, and clout to keep the process going.

In the upcoming chapters, we will examine these roles and the skills needed to excel in them.

Notes

1. Thomas J. Peters and Robert H. Waterman, Jr., *In Search of Excellence* (New York: Warner Books, 1982), p. 168.
2. G. Lynn Shostack, "Designing Services that Deliver," *Harvard Business Review,* January–February 1984.
3. W. Earl Sasser, "Match Supply and Demand in Service Industries," *Harvard Business Review,* November–December 1976.

Eleven

Step 6: Becoming a Customer-Champion

As a Customer-Champion, the first of the new management roles, you act as the eyes, ears, and voice of the customer. Even though you personally may never see customers, you need to represent them in your organization. You "think customer" whenever you make a decision or establish a policy; you use your clout as a manager to learn what customers want and see to it that their requirements are met.

We repeat: Service excellence—however you measure it—is a matter of meeting your customers' requirements. And you can't meet these requirements if you don't know what they are. Not what you *think* they are or what you *hope* they are, but what they really are.

These days, you cannot predict what customers want. As Regis McKenna says, "When we see wealthy people driving Volkswagens and pickup trucks, it becomes clear that this is a society where individual tastes are no longer predictable; marketers cannot easily and neatly categorize their customer base." [1]

At this point, you have your customer information system in place. What else can you, the Customer-Champion, do?

Well, of course, you can get out and meet customers, talk to them at the point of service to find out what's on their mind. You can experience what they experience by going through your service cycle yourself. You can visit customers regularly to learn what they're thinking and how they rate your service. Put yourself in their shoes: what would you think of your service if you were they?

Just as you act as the customers' eyes and ears in being a Customer-Champion, you also act as their voice.

Some organizations have a customer service department that is in reality the complaint department. The people who staff this department are supposed to function as customer advocates; instead they hear only the negative side of things. But we're not talking about just *re*acting to customers; we're talking pro-action—building the customer's voice into all your decisions, learning what customers want, delivering it to them, and solving problems before customers come to you when something goes wrong.

So every manager needs to push for what's best for customers, because without them, the organization will cease to exist.

Voting With Your Feet

How much of your day do you presently spend in the role of Customer-Champion? If you want your employees to learn the behavior of customer-driven service, you need to model it personally. Employees seldom "read the lips" of their managers. They've learned that this doesn't always tell the whole story. So they watch your feet: Where do you spend your time? What meetings do you attend or skip? Where do you travel? What do you value? What, in other words, do they need to do to get ahead in your company?

To evaluate what "your feet" are doing, complete the Decision/Action Log in Worksheet 23, which cover your decisions in a typical day in your office.

Then, in each set of four boxes, enter a +, −, or ? according to the effect this decision has on subordinates, peers, direct customers, and ultimate customers. A plus (+) means a positive effect; a minus (−) means a negative effect; a question mark (?) means you don't have enough information.

For example, suppose you decided to charge for something that was previously free (e.g., training customers on how to use your computers). This could have a positive effect on subordinates, who might have more time for other things; a negative effect on peers, who will suffer from complaints about the new charges; a negative effect on your direct (internal) customers, the documentation staff, who will have to provide clearer manuals. But unless you've talked to some of your ultimate customers about it, you don't know the effect on them.

To score:

1. Put the total number of decisions for the day on the bottom left.
2. Count the total number of positives in each column and enter it in the bottom right.

What can you conclude about the effect of your decisions and the kind of decisions you are making?

(text continues on page 140)

Worksheet 23. Decision/Action Log

Date:

List every action or decision you accomplished on this day to learn how much time you now spend as a Customer-Champion.

	Subordinates	Peers	Direct Customers	Ultimate Customers
1	☐	☐	☐	☐
2	☐	☐	☐	☐
3	☐	☐	☐	☐
4	☐	☐	☐	☐
5	☐	☐	☐	☐
6	☐	☐	☐	☐
7	☐	☐	☐	☐
8	☐	☐	☐	☐
9	☐	☐	☐	☐
10	☐	☐	☐	☐
11	☐	☐	☐	☐
12	☐	☐	☐	☐
13	☐	☐	☐	☐

Total Decisions _____   Total + ☐ ☐ ☐ ☐

Reprinted by courtesy of Learning Dynamics, Inc.

Customer Impact Statements

All of your systems, policies, and decisions send messages to customers. Are they friendly? Or do they send "We don't trust you" or "We're adversaries" or "You're a pest" messages?

Customer-Champions pay close attention to these messages, because this is precisely where you win or lose with your customers. So examine every decision from your customers' point of view to learn its impact—positive or negative.

For example, suppose you are a bank officer who decides from now on that all customers must provide two forms of identification to cash a check. The positive impact on customers is unknown. The negative impact will likely be that lines will be slower and customers will be annoyed and insulted at being treated like bandits.

Or take a decision to raise prices. Obviously there is going to be a negative impact; few customers like paying more money. But perhaps you can find a positive impact in that these prices will allow you to provide better service.

To be truly customer-driven, from now on, determine the impact of all your key decisions. We're not saying to make every decision based on what customers want (they don't always know what they want). But don't fly blind. Evaluate the effect on customers of every key decision you make.

First Chicago Bank does this now. It calls its decision process a "customer focus mandate" and reports, "Before you make a change, you *must* take the customer viewpoint."[2]

Similarly, prior to any major construction project, the U.S. Environmental Protection Agency requires that developers do an environmental impact study of the project's effect on the surrounding area.

For each major decision, answer these questions:

1. What is the decision to be made, and what are the options?
2. Who are the customers, customer types, or market segments likely to be affected by the decision?
3. What are the impacts, positive and negative, of each option on each market segment?

You can complete the customer impact statement in Worksheet 24, which plugs the customer into your decision-making loop. Too often, we forget whom we work for. A customer impact statement keeps your eye firmly on your "ultimate boss."

Worksheet 24. Customer Impact Statement

Date: [   ]

Evaluate the probable impact on customers (internal and external) of each major decision you are about to make. Put a + if the impact will be positive, a − if it will be negative, and a ? if you are unsure.

	Subordinates	Peers	Direct Customers	Ultimate Customers
1.	☐	☐	☐	☐
2.	☐	☐	☐	☐
3.	☐	☐	☐	☐

Reprinted by courtesy of Learning Dynamics, Inc.

Customer Service Opportunities

Customer Service Opportunities (CSOs) are what distinguish the successful company from the industry leader. CSOs represent a way of serving customers better at very little cost. They give you a chance to add value—to exceed customers' requirements with personal touches that go beyond what they expect.

Capitalizing on CSOs also allows you to raise customer expectations beyond the capability of your competitors. Furthermore, the more your product looks like a commodity, the more valuable CSOs become. Remember, you cannot afford a single dissatisfied customer. And exploiting CSOs leads to a constantly growing market share. Conversely, *exploiting customers* leads to the "death spiral." (You'll lose customers, which will cause you to cut costs, which will lead to more lost customers, which will lead to. . . .)

Here are some examples of companies that saw an opportunity to serve their customers and took it.

Grocery shoppers often complain about difficulties in finding items in the store or adjusting recipes or getting coupons for items they don't need. The Kroger stores in Cincinnati turned these complaints into CSOs and installed computers that can:

- Show shoppers exactly where in the store to find an item
- Print recipes, adjusting the proportions to the number of servings you want
- Print cents-off coupons for the items in the recipe

To capitalize on a CSO, you need a "whatever it takes to keep customers happy" attitude. Unusual requests from customers are not seen as disruptions but as opportunities to add value.

For example, the Polaroid Corporation interprets warranties liberally, trains customers on how to use cameras at its repair facilities, and offers loaners if cameras have to be in the shop for more than a few days.[3]

To find CSOs, don't look at customer complaints as problems but as opportunities to serve the public better than your competition.

Host International, a division of the Marriott Corporation that operates airport facilities, found that customers rated their restaurants' food and prices poorly. Yet the same food would get higher marks away from the airport. Puzzled over these facts, company executives decided to look on the dining experience from the customer's point of view. They realized that air travelers were not in a positive frame of mind when they entered a Host International Restaurant; they were rushed, tired, and perhaps angry about poor service they had received elsewhere.

Host decided that instead of trying to upgrade food or lower prices, it would work on service, "offering the customer a total service package."[4]

Try the "Complaints as Opportunities" on yourself by completing Worksheet 25.

What Customers Want

To find CSOs, consider what customers want. Needs are many and complex, but they often come down to these ten.

1. *Customers want to be treated with dignity and respect.* Do you have rules that belittle them?
2. *Customers want your product or service to meet their expectations.* Are you giving them realistic expectations? How do you deal with unrealistic expectations?
3. *Customers want to be successful.* How do your customers feel after dealing with you?
4. *Customers want help with their problems.* How do you suggest alter-

Worksheet 25. Complaints as Opportunities

A. Think of a recent *negative* service experience you've had as a customer. Describe it briefly below.

_____

_____

_____

_____

B. List three possible Customer Service Opportunities in that interaction.

1. _____

_____

_____

2. _____

_____

_____

3. _____

_____

_____

Reprinted by courtesy of Learning Dynamics, Inc.

natives, bend the rules to help, and steer customers away from further problems?

5. *Customers want to be treated as individuals with unique needs.* How can you motivate your people to be genuinely interested in customers?

6. *Customers want you to observe their self image.* How do you treat customers? (as mature adults; smart businesspeople; children; liars?)

7. *Customers want you to respect their time.* How quickly do you respond to customers?

8. *Customers want someone on their side.* Do your customers feel your contact people are on their side, or are they part of a stone wall?

9. *Customers want information.* How accessible and clear is information on procedures and new services?

10. *Customers want benefits from buying.* What's in it for customers who use your service?

Finding CSOs

Here are some suggestions on how to find CSOs.

1. Look for areas that are now mature or dominated by big companies. These markets are likely to be ripe for a creative competitor to find new ways of providing service.

For example, every working person has probably felt the frustration of deliveries that can be made only during "normal business hours." Lazarus, a regional department store, offers evening deliveries.[5]

Another common frustration is not having furniture available when you're ready to move in. Herman Miller Inc. furniture offers guaranteed move-in dates, as well as five-year warranties.[6]

2. Listen to your customers, ex-customers, and noncustomers. Use every available channel: formal surveys, informal listening, etc. They'll tell you what they're not getting now.

For example, WaterMaster (Columbus, Ohio) turned complaints into a customer service opportunity. Building owners, who pay each of their buildings' water bills themselves, complain that some tenants use a lot more water than others, but they can't tell which ones. WaterMaster offers to install water "submeters" in buildings, so landlords can track and bill tenants individually for water usage.

3. Ask customers how they use your product or service now. You may find some uses you never thought of that will lead to CSOs.

For example, Euramerica (New York City) is a technical translation service specializing in advertisements. Founder Yuri Radzievsky, a Soviet emigre, noticed the poor use his translations were being put to, so he expanded his services to include graphics, typesetting, audiovisuals, and consulting. (Sensitivity to other cultures can prevent mistakes like one company's ad, "Be sure to use our heavy-duty mouth detergent every morning.")

American Standard realized that Americans were spending more time at home. What could the manufacturer of a commodity like bathroom fixtures do about this? It designed a bathroom that doubles as a home entertainment center, with features like closed-circuit TV to enable the homeowner to see who's at the door and individual bathwater temperatures that family members can pre-set.[7]

4. Ask your employees how customers are using your product/service—and not just high customer-contact people like sales and service. Purchasing, accounting, training, and MIS folks probably have ideas, too.

5. Study your cycle of service flowchart (Worksheet 22 in Chapter 10) for places to improve service or to add value in ways that set you apart from your competition. Satisfying one CSO will lead to other CSOs.

Meeting a need creates other needs, as when IBM branched out into hardware and software.

Complete the personal action in Worksheet 26 to identify as many CSOs in your company or department as possible.

Your Department's CSOs

We've been talking about how an organization finds CSOs, but what about your department?

All work is a process. You get inputs, process them, and produce output. "Adding value" means your output is worth more than your inputs:

Inputs	Process	Outputs
Information	Procedures	Service
Materials	People	Product
	Equipment	
	Energy	

What value do you add to customers? If you're not sure, turn the question around: If your department disappeared tomorrow, what effect would it have on customers? Would they notice you'd disappeared? If the answer is "none" or "no," your function may be in trouble.

A final reason to act as Customer-Champion: Sometimes the only person who knows the whole cycle of service is your customer! As managers, we're so concerned with our management functions that we often only pay attention to repairs, billing, order-taking, and costs, and miss seeing the big picture. So listen to your customers to see how they experience your service, and you'll find opportunities for improvement.

Worksheet 26. Spotting CSOs

1. Identify as many CSOs in your company as possible. Use your log sheet, your company's marketing materials, and your mission statement as idea triggers.

(continues)

Worksheet 26 (*continued*)

_____

_____

_____

_____

_____

_____

_____

_____

2. In the space below, develop action plans for exploiting the three most important CSOs.

CSO: _____

Plan: _____

_____

_____

_____

CSO: _____

Plan: _____

_____

_____

_____

CSO: _____

Plan: _____

_____

_____

_____

Notes

1. Regis McKenna, "Marketing in an Age of Diversity," *Harvard Business Review,* September 1988, p. 88.
2. Learning Dynamics survey.
3. John Lane, "Identifying Service Objectives," in Jay Sprechler, *When America Does It Right* (Norcross, Ga.: Industrial Engineering and Management Press, 1988), pp. 414–416.
4. Karl Albrecht, *At America's Service* (Homewood, Ill.: Dow Jones-Irwin, 1988), p. 160.
5. Daniel G. Bukey, "The Lazarus Customer Service Evolution," in Sprechler, p. 450.
6. Ray Pukanic and Dick Holm, "The Herman Miller Quality Audit: A Corporate Report Card," in Sprechler, p. 177.
7. Tom Peters, "America . . . Beyond the Search for Excellence" seminar, Management Communications Inc., Boston, 1988.

Twelve

Step 7: Employee Motivation and Self-Esteem

Another face of customer-driven management, and your second major role, is Coach-Counselor. This role requires helping your subordinates to meet customers' requirements: to be Customer-Champions and Customer Problem-solvers on their own.

Being a Coach-Counselor starts with meeting employees' own needs—for knowledge, resources, and empowerment—so they can serve customers better. And it includes building employees' self-esteem.

Why this is helpful to customers, and how you do it, brings us to the seventh step in the strategy: building employee motivation, commitment, and self-esteem.

You can be the Coach-Counselor in an informal way, so long as you are consistent. Or you can establish a formal system, as do many companies. However you do it, you need a way to deal with people problems in areas like motivation, job satisfaction, skills training, and career growth. By dealing with these employee concerns, you prevent problems with your customers.

Yes, that's what we said—prevent problems with *customers.*

This is one of the most profound ideas we can give you. If you take nothing else from this book, take this, because without it, nothing else you do will work for long: *Customer relations mirror employee relations. The way you treat your employees is the way they will treat your customers.* This idea stems from research by Citicorp that studied 112 top service organizations. The study concluded, "If management solves employee problems, employees solve customers' problems. It is as simple as that."[1]

In practice, it means that the way you treat employees is how those employees will treat customers. If you are indifferent to your employees, they will be indifferent to customers. If you keep them in the dark about your values and what's happening in your organization, they won't know enough to take responsibility or to help customers. If you avoid customers and treat them like pests, so will your employees. If you put costs, systems, and rules ahead of meeting your customers' needs, so will your employees.

The Customer/Employee Relationship Mirror

Figure 12-1 shows how the messages you send employees get translated to customers.[2]

What Are Your Problems and How Can I Help Solve Them?

How can you and your organization show you care about employee problems? Here are some ideas:

- Some managers have no doors on their offices, symbolizing the fact that if you have a problem, you can go directly to the person who can solve it.
- Some have regular meetings in which top management solicits suggestions from rank and file.
- Some companies sponsor employee assistance programs, day care centers, and credit unions as ways of showing concern for employees' needs.
- Marriott, one of the frontrunners in this area, has long had programs to support employees, including an ombudsman service, career ladders, and profit sharing. Chairman Willard Marriott says: "My job is to motivate [subordinates], teach them, help them, and care about them."[3] His motto: "Take care of your employees and they'll take care of your customers."[4]

Does this mean that management bends to every subordinate whim? No, because employees want well-run organizations with clear, consistent rules. Employees, like all people, like to know where they stand.

We Want You to Know What Is Happening in Our Organization

Companies like Delta and GE bring all employees together in small groups to discuss the state of the business. What kind of company information can you share?

- Overall picture of sales, profits, new products and services, competition

Figure 12-1. Customer/employee relationship mirror.

Organization to Employee	Employee to Customer
What are your problems and how can I help solve them?	How may I *help* you?
We want you to know what is happening in our organization.	I can help you because I know what's going on.
We're all part of the company, so we're all responsible for what happens here.	I have the authority to help you, and I'm proud of my ability to do it.
We treat each other with professional respect.	I value you as an individual.
We stand behind each other's decisions and support each other.	You can count on me and my company to deliver on our promises.

Reprinted by courtesy of Learning Dynamics, Inc.

- Activities of other divisions and departments
- Update on progress toward goals and celebrations of achievements

GE believes if every employee knows what is happening in the organization, every customer encounter will benefit the company, even those employees not in customer service. It never wants an employee to say "I don't know" or "It's not my job." (If an employee doesn't know, he or she can quickly find out or put the customer in touch with someone who does know.)[5]

We're All Part of the Company, So We're All Responsible for What Happens Here

In successful service-driven companies, this spirit of collective responsibility starts with the orientation of new employees. They learn their responsibilities to other employees and to customers—and that they are accountable for their behavior. It continues by routing customer comments, good and bad, back to the responsible employee, making accountability part of performance reviews, and publicly rewarding employees who go out of their way to serve the customer.

At Nordstrom's monthly meetings, managers read customer letters aloud to cheering staff. Salespeople praised in these letters are "Customer Service All-Stars." They have their picture hung next to the customer service desk, receive added discounts on clothing, and get notes placed in their personnel files.[6]

We Treat Each Other With Professional Respect

How can managers show respect? Here are some possibilities:

- Praising a job well done
- Calling employees by the names they prefer
- Reprimanding only in private
- Providing clean facilities
- Saying "please" and "thank you"
- Listening to, and trying to understand, employees' opinions

Employees who don't feel respected are touchy with difficult customers. Those treated with respect have a longer fuse.

We Stand Behind Each Other's Decisions and Support Each Other

Employees perform better when their boss supports them. By "support," we mean:

- Providing the staffing, resources, and knowledge they need to do their job effectively
- Giving fair pay increases
- Accepting responsibility for subordinates' mistakes
- Defending subordinates in front of others
- Focusing on correcting problems, rather than pinpointing blame

A supportive boss keeps his or her promises to subordinates so they in turn know that they can make promises to customers that the company will keep.

Here's an example of supporting subordinates:

> Attention all units: Wanda may be in the building.
>
> —Public announcement,
> National Aquarium in Baltimore

What follows is a case example for all executives who believe that:

1. You can't provide quality customer service with "the entry-level people who are available at the rates we pay."
2. Spending money to train entry-level, part-time, or volunteer employees is throwing money down a rat hole.

Wanda Draper is director of community affairs and visitor services— and in charge of just about everything except the fish at the National

Aquarium in Baltimore. Wanda says her mission is "to help ensure a quality museum that is an international leader in aquatic education and entertainment."

One of her big challenges is to compete for staff with the city's revitalized showcase area, Inner Harbor Center. Average wages there are considerably higher than the National Aquarium rate.

Wanda believes most of the support staff (ticket-takers, security, administrative, gift shop, and maintenance staff) are attracted by the mystique of the aquarium. She also credits the area's easy accessibility to public transportation and a staff kitchen with a microwave, which helps defray the high cost of meals in the posh tourist section, with helping attract personnel.

Perhaps. But after hearing her describe her management style and after seeing firsthand her obsessive commitment to service quality, we're inclined to believe Wanda makes the mystique.

Some of her management practices are just common sense. She learns everyone's name and uses it—no small feat with thirty part- and full-time staff members and sixty seasonal people. She keeps her office door open; people can come in, or even call her at home, if they have a problem. And she walks around the facility frequently, being especially careful to do so "when things are going well." She doesn't want to be seen as an inspector but as a resource and a champion for her employees.

Although she constantly models and communicates the importance of caring for aquarium guests, she will not allow her people to suffer abuse. Some of her solutions to customer/guest problems would qualify her for King Solomon's job, but her message to employees is clear: "Your manager backs you up."

Her people believe her: During her museum walks, an employee may warn her, "You're going to get a nasty letter from a visitor." That's okay with Wanda because she knows she'll get the employee's side of the story through an incident report. Most likely, she'll back up the employee, even banning obnoxious visitors from the aquarium. If things get really nasty (most often with tour groups), the staff can depend on Wanda somehow learning about it and appearing in person to take care of it.

Training at the aquarium is ongoing. One aspect focuses on "product knowledge": how to answer guest questions like, "How many gallons in that tank?" "Where do the puffins come from?" "Are the whales happy here?"

The other part of training focuses on service excellence, from awareness of each person's importance in the process to skills in listening, problem-solving, valuing customers, and dealing with the personal stress that handling 1.4 million visitors a year can bring.

Wanda tells this story with obvious pride and pleasure: She'd left the building for the day and, after dinner, returned to pick up something from her office. Someone evidently spotted her car and wanted the entire

Worksheet 27. Your Organization's Mirror

Analyze your organization/group's typical messages to determine what employees mirror to customers. Then develop new, changed messages where needed.

Message to Employees   Translation to Customers   Changed Message

Reprinted by courtesy of Learning Dynamics, Inc.

staff to be on its toes and qualified for Wanda's generous praise. As Wanda entered the side entrance, she heard over the loudspeaker, "Attention all units: Wanda may be in the building." Visitors, of course, thought it was an aquarium joke.*

The moral for managers is clear: *Walk what you talk.* Treat employees the way you want them to treat your customers.

How are you doing? Try Worksheet 27, "Your Organization's Mirror." Based on your knowledge as a manager, what are the messages your organization sends to employees? How are they being translated to customers? How will the messages need to change?

Your Portfolio

Let's supply the dollar and cents reasons for treating employees well. The numbers in Figure 12-2 are based on a projection of an express delivery driver.[7]

*The movie "A Fish Called Wanda" had just come out.

Figure 12-2.   Your portfolio: example.

A projection of the dollar impact on an express delivery driver:

Amount average customer spends yearly	$18,000
× number of years per good customer	10
= average value of account	$180,000
× number of accounts visited daily	40
= accounts handled by typical driver	$7.2 million
× minimum people each customer tells	2
= value each driver responsible for	$14.4 million

Reprinted by courtesy of Learning Dynamics, Inc.

As astonishing as these numbers seem, they are conservative. The "minimum number of people each customer tells" is more like ten, according to a U.S. Office of Consumer Affairs study.[8]

Now turn to Worksheet 28 and do the calculations for someone in your organization who interacts with customers.

One company that is especially committed to meeting the self-esteem needs of its employees is Bell Atlantic. Under the guidance of Vada Miller (since retired) and Barbra McKenzie, the company's operator services division has undertaken the daunting task of building the customer satisfaction skills, as well as the confidence and self-esteem, of operators handling eight billion customer calls per year.

All 12,500 of these directory assistance and call completion (toll-assistance) operators have had technical training, and many have had bits and pieces of customer courtesy training. Still, despite the famous Bell team spirit, most operators didn't feel very important in the overall scheme of things.

New Trends Driving Customer Satisfaction

Following the 1984 breakup of AT&T, Bell Atlantic recognized and acknowledged that "operators are the most important employees we have; they are the company" (company slogan). At the same time, new technology, diversification, and intense new competition made customer satisfaction ratings a top priority.

Worksheet 28. Your People's Portfolio

How much business can your subordinates affect? To determine the vale of someone who interacts with customers, calculate the following:

Amount average customer spends yearly	$	
Times number of years per good customer	×	
Equals average value of account	= $	
Times average number of customers each subordinate contacts yearly	×	
Equals value handled by each person	= $	

Reprinted by courtesy of Learning Dynamics, Inc.

Telephone customers are prospects for new products and services. If operators treat them badly, they may well go elsewhere. As a result, a major system-wide shift in operator training is under way—in Barbra McKenzie's words from "This is how to use the equipment" to "Use your judgment, listen to customers, add value to our services."

Using their own judgment on the job is a big step for most operators, who don't yet fully understand the changed role they will play in the restructured, revitalized Bell Atlantic of the year 2000. And building customer contact skills, self-esteem, and confidence into a short customer encounter might seem farfetched. But the payoff has been dramatic and immediate. At C&P Telephone, where the pilot program "Putting the Customer 1st" was conducted, customer satisfaction ratings rose from 92 to 96.4, after just one training session. Now rolling out through the entire system, the program seems to promise a large payoff for Bell Atlantic's long-term commitment to employee development.

Employees as Customers and Suppliers—The Value Chain

So far we've been talking about serving your ultimate customers, the people who purchase your product or service.

And, as we've seen, the ultimate user is not your only customer. Your customer is also anyone for whom you produce work, often people in the next department.

"Customer" also includes your employees. For them to do their job most effectively, they need certain things from you: information, resources, support, empowerment.

This point becomes clear when you look at work flow.

Let's look at this in terms of a value chain (Figure 12-3).

By comparison, on an assembly line, where everyone may be 99 percent accurate, and you have 100 steps. By the end of the line, as we pointed out in Chapter 6, you only have 36 percent accuracy. The further back in the chain you are, the more impact you have. Take training, for example: If the trainer is only 90 percent efficient with the first worker and everybody else is still 95 percent right, by the end of five steps you're down to 73 percent.

One way to improve accuracy is to cut the number of steps between you and the customer, which is another way of saying, "Get closer to your customer."

What about you? Who are your customers and suppliers? From what internal departments do you get input and for which do you produce output? Chart your work flow and then identify your customers and suppliers in your value chain—in Worksheet 29.

Meeting Value Chain Requirements

Since you produce outputs like these for your subordinates, you need to know their requirements. When you give them what they need, they can do the job for which you hired them.

When you look on yourself as a supplier to your employees, you discover that it's necessary to learn their requirements and what it will take to satisfy these internal customers.

Remember, when customers contact your front line, they see that person as your whole company. This is a powerful reason to be serving and supplying your contact people really well.

To act in your Coach-Counselor role:

- Regularly ask your people what you can do to help them do their job better.
- Provide as much training for their job as your budget allows.
- Constantly think of ways you can make their job easier (reprogramming, restructuring relationships, revising systems, bringing in new technology).
- Meet regularly with your people to review your effectiveness and get suggestions.
- Stop wasting their time. Eliminate paperwork that nobody really needs and throw out rules that only serve to exert power.

The better you treat your employees, the better they will treat customers. For example, a study of hotels[9] found that those that had the least turnover:

Figure 12-3.   The value chain.

All work consists of taking input, processing it, and producing output. At each step, the person from whom you get input is your supplier, the person for whom you produce output is your customer, until the output reaches the ultimate consumer. And each customer has requirements the supplier needs to meet.

The value chain represents the links between you and the customer:

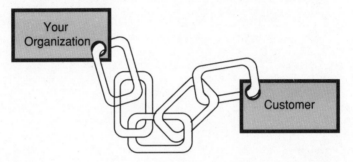

If each link in the chain meets requirements 95 percent of the time, the impact is this:

Step	1	2	3	4	5
Accuracy	95%	95%	95%	95%	95%
Cumulative Accuracy	95%	90%	86%	81%	77%

Reprinted by courtesy of Learning Dynamics, Inc.

- Improved job status by reducing paperwork and bottlenecks
- Redecorated and improved physical working conditions to relieve crowding and improve privacy
- Used pay to reward both loyalty and superior performance
- Made hours more reasonable
- Fired poor workers, which good performers appreciated

Since customer relations mirror employee relations, let's look at some ways of satisfying your employees.

Worksheet 29. Your Value Chain

Determine your internal and external requirements at each step of your work process.

Input	Process	Process	Process	Process	Output
_____	_____	_____	_____	_____	_____
	Require-ments	Require-ments	Require-ments	Require-ments	Require-ments
	_____	_____	_____	_____	_____
	_____	_____	_____	_____	_____
	_____	_____	_____	_____	_____

Supplier	Input	Customer
_____	_____	_____
_____	_____	_____
_____	_____	_____
_____	_____	_____
_____	_____	_____

Just as you need to find out what each external customer wants, you need to learn what motivates each employee, because each is different. Most managers are familiar with Maslow's Hierarchy of Needs, which holds that once our basic needs are met, we are motivated to seek other things. So, too, different employees are on different motivation levels. As Coach-Counselor, you attempt to learn where and what it will take to motivate each employee.

For example, Edward Link, president of Link-Allen & Associates of San Mateo, California spends several hours at the beginning of each year with the top 10 percent of employees—those he can least afford to lose. He asks them what they really need. Answers range from more life insurance to a new car to more time with the boss.[10]

Career Growth

Not all contact people want to advance. But some do, and helping them get ahead is a motivator. Ask them where they want to go so you can help them build a career ladder.

Even those not interested in advancement can tell you their goals, giving you the information you need to help them achieve success in their own terms.

Some other ways to motivate employees are:

- Training
- Getting employees involved in decision making
- Knowing rank-and-file staff's names
- Featuring employees in ads, annual reports, newsletters
- Communicating rewards for meeting goals and standards in company publications

Critiquing Performance

Finally, as part of your Coach-Counselor role, you need to correct poor performance. To serve customers well, employees need to know how they're doing, with feedback from you—both positive and not-so-positive. When you do need to correct poor or unacceptable behavior, do so constructively, rather than kill motivation just because people need correcting.

Here are some suggestions:

1. When you are out on the line, pay close attention to how employees are interacting with customers. See for yourself, rather than getting things secondhand.

2. Be lavish with praise. It costs nothing, and the payoff is enormous—for your employees and your customers.

What are some general areas to praise that will impact positively on customers? Here are a few:

- Exceeding performance standards
- Consistently meeting standards
- Showing any improvement, no matter how small
- Staying calm with a difficult customer
- Going out of one's way to help someone

Remember, the first law of human behavior states, "Any behavior that is immediately reinforced or rewarded will tend to be repeated."

This means that when you praise people, they associate the praise with what they did just before it, so they are likely to do it again.

3. When you correct employees, do it in a valuing way—and always in private.

Figure 12-4. Critiquing poor performance.

What to Do

Consider feelings of employees
Cool down, analyze each situation
Show confidence in the employee's ability to make necessary changes
Carefully explain the nature of any violation and the correction expected
Always reprimand in private
Outline specific consequences of future violations, and follow through
Give every employee fair treatment
Give prompt attention to violations
Define objectives of disciplinary action
Deal promptly with all violations of the rules

What to Avoid

Sarcasm
Loss of temper
Humiliating an employee
Profanity
Public reprimands
Threats and bluffs
Showing favoritism
Delay tactics
Unduly harsh penalties
Inconsistent enforcement

Reprinted by courtesy of Learning Dynamics, Inc.

Some do's and don'ts for critiquing people constructively are in Figure 12-4.

In summary, the fact that you are providing a service is both a challenge and an opportunity—a challenge because people vary so much that you can't regulate them like you can machines, and an opportunity because, with this difference, you can harness each individual's creative energy to provide excellent customer care on a one-to-one basis.

Employees need to feel good about management, the company values, and customers. You're not dealing with a production line that you can fix with statistical process control. Service consists of two people interacting. To the customer, the customer service representative *is* the company. And if the CSR feels bad—or sees you treat customers like pests—the customer will be poorly served.

Notes

1. Robert Desatnick, *Managing to Keep the Customer* (San Francisco: Jossey-Bass, 1987), Ch. 2.
2. *Ibid.*
3. Ron Zemke, *Service Excellence Workbook* (Waltham, Mass.: Performance Research Associates, 1986), p. 31.
4. Karl Albrecht, *At America's Service* (Homewood, Ill.: Dow Jones-Irwin, 1987), p. 41.
5. Desatnick, *Managing to Keep the Customer.*
6. Robert W. Stevenson, "Retail Rebel," *The New York Times Magazine*, August 27, 1989.
7. Tom Peters, *Thriving on Chaos* (New York: Knopf, 1988), p. 98.
8. TARP (Technical Assistance Research Programs Institute), "Consumer Complaint Handling in America: An Update Study" (Washington, D.C.: U.S. Office of Consumer Affairs, 1986).
9. William Wasmuth and Stanley Davis, "Strategies for Managing Employee Turnover," *Cornell H.R.A. Quarterly*, August 1983.
10. "Keeping Key People Happy," *Inc.*, October 1987, p. 140.

Thirteen

Step 8: Empowerment and Training

As we've seen, learning the role of Customer-Champion means you become the eyes, ears, and voice of your customers to better meet their needs. Even though you personally may never see customers, as a Customer-Champion you represent them within your organization. You are responsible for the policies, systems, and decisions that affect customers and the 80 percent of customer problems that these policies, systems, and decisions create. But you need help.

To integrate the process, you need employees who are empowered with the authority to respond, and trained in the skills to act for customers. In short, you need Customer-Champions throughout your organization.

So another most important step in the master strategy—the component that makes customer-driven service happen—is empowering and training your people.

Here's a horror story to make the point:

Recently, *Marketing News* made 5,000 calls to business advertisers in the Yellow Pages, requesting price information. Here are the results they recorded:

Did not answer in the first eight rings	56%
Put the caller on hold for more than two minutes	8%
Couldn't provide the price information requested	11%
Provided only the price and then hung up	34%
Did not even ask the caller's name	78%

Would you say that these 5,000 companies needed to train their people? And do you think it would pay off?

There is little doubt that people are the key ingredient in a customer-driven organization: you, top and middle managers, CSRs, supervisors, professionals, accountants, salespeople, receptionists, telephone answerers, data processors, truck drivers.

Everyone in the place needs to support and execute the goal.

Here are the key reasons for empowering and training people at all levels to take care of your customers:

- To gain commitment and support
- To integrate companywide service quality goals
- To teach service quality skills and principles
- To convince all employees that customer care is their job
- To emphasize the importance of people's different roles in the overall company program, particularly those who don't interface with customers
- To increase participation, motivation, and self-esteem of people at every level in the organization

Empowering Decision-Makers and Problem-Solvers

Our employees manage to get up on time, drive their own cars, fix dinner, buy houses, and raise children. Can't we trust them to make decisions at work?

If we treat them like two-year olds, that's the behavior they're going to mirror to customers. but if we treat them as responsible adults, chances are they'll behave responsibly with customers.

This doesn't mean you let employees do whatever they want (although Nordstrom's department stores is tremendously successful with only one sentence in its employee handbook: "Use your good judgment in all situations").

It means that you show employees, through behavior modeling, policies, training, and reward systems, what customer-driven service means. Then you empower them to make decisions for which they're accountable.

For example, Dick Scott, chief operating officer of Long's Drug Stores, noticed that his managers were approving each customer's check. He suggested that the function be turned over to cashiers.

His managers thought this would be too risky because they used a lot of part-timers and teenagers. Scott asked one manager what thought process he used when approving a check. The answer: None—he just checked a driver's license. Scott replied, "Well, it shouldn't be too hard for us to train these people to do it."

The change had three effects:

1. Customers liked the stores better. Not having to wait for the manager sped up the check-out process. Customers also felt trusted this way.
2. The bad check rate stayed the same.
3. Cashiers felt more responsible and trusted.

There is little question that empowering people who serve customers improves your customers' view of your service quality. And statistics show that empowerment actually saves money. Let's look at an example.

Let's say the average cost to issue full credit on a complaint is $50. Let's also say that it probably costs about $25 to investigate a complaint before issuing credit and that in two-thirds of the cases, you'll issue a full credit. Here's what the numbers would look like:[1]

Pay off all complaints	$50.00
Investigate all complaints	$25.00
Pay off 2/3 of complaints ($50 × 2/3)	$33.33
Average cost to investigate/resolve complaint	$58.33

You actually save the company $8 each time if subordinates are empowered to pay off small complaints. Also, since most customers really are honest, you'll gain many times $50 in goodwill and reputation by settling on the spot.

Furthermore, research shows that if you do solve a customer's problem without haggling, more than 90 percent will forget the problem and continue to do business.[2] Only 70 percent of customers stay with you if their problems have to be referred to managers and then take days or weeks to resolve.

As Rosabeth Moss Kanter of Harvard says, "In large organizations at least, I have observed that powerlessness 'corrupts.'. . . ."[3] That is, it leads to defensiveness rather than cooperation. She further states, "To produce results, power—like money—needs to circulate."[4]

Directed Autonomy

Let's say you agree in principle with the idea of empowerment. How do you put it into the picture? Not to be wiseacres, but the answer is, "With difficulty."

For employees, it calls for a process called "directed autonomy." You set standards and guidelines within which employees operate and train them in problem solving (more on this in the next chapter). Don't put them in a straightjacket.

At U.S. West (one of the former AT&T regional companies), "employees are empowered to make many decisions on their own, because the customer is more important than the rules. Instead of Wednesday installation, the company will schedule appointments for 3 P.M. Wednesday—or even 3 A.M."[5]

Home Federal Savings and Loan of California believes "high-quality service is simply unattainable *unless* the authority to resolve client complaints has been firmly and irrevocably placed in the hands of the front-line employee on the spot. Client-contact personnel must know that they have the authority to act and must know that they cannot be second-guessed . . .

"There is no formula, suitable for recitation by rote or for plastering on a wall in poster form, that will tell front-line personnel what to do or will unerringly guide their judgments. It is a one-to-one transaction and can only be guided by training and by corporate values effectively communicated . . .

"Front-line decisions must be upheld all the way up the line, even when mistakes are made. . . . If the burden of decision falls on the front line, the burden of support rests at every link in the chain of command."[6]

But giving away power is difficult for many managers—even on a controlled basis like directed autonomy. This means managers need training too.

The Fuel That Feeds the Fire—Training Your Staff to Deliver Customer-Driven Service

At this point, it is probably clear that training—learning new behaviors, attitudes, and skills—is the fuel that feeds this entire process.

Without the necessary training—from top to bottom—the change in corporate culture is unlikely to occur. This is so because everyone needs to know not only what to do but also how to do it. And everyone needs to be motivated and committed.

Training takes place on four levels as follows:

1. *Top executives* are trained in customer-driven management strategies and learn the skills needed to power and model a service-driven corporate culture.

2. *Managers and supervisors* need training in customer championship, empowerment, team building, and Coach-Counseling to learn their roles

and the skills necessary to integrate the program throughout the organization. Such training is compulsory in many of the best organizations.

3. *Front-line customer contact* people learn the attitudes, strategies, and skills of helping, fixing, and putting the customer's needs first. Too often these people feel, "Don't bother me, I have work to do." These feelings get translated into attitudes and behaviors that turn customers away.

4. *Everyone else in the company* completes a core program in service quality awareness. This shows all employees the benefits of service excellence to the company and to their own career. It impresses them with their individual importance in the process, helps them understand the "internal customer" process, and helps gain their support and commitment.

Many top executives have learned to their surprise and disappointment that halfway measures to promote customer care—slogans, wall posters, and advertising pitches—produce short-lived results at best.

Managers—be they top, middle, or frontline—cannot just give lip service to the idea, to say, in effect, "Be customer-friendly and service-driven," and then slam the door to their office.

As we've said repeatedly, subordinates base their behavior on what their managers do, not on what they say. When they see their manager spending time at the customer service desk or praising employees for the wonderful way they dealt with a difficult customer, congratulating the group or distributing small rewards for meeting service quality goals—this is what will motivate them.

Few managers understand the powerful impact their behavior has on their subordinates. Managers need to learn this, as well as their roles and their behaviors in producing a service-driven culture. They need to focus on customers and to "think customer" in their decisions. And they need to learn the skills of training and developing others to care for customers as well.

Keep in mind that most managers today are managing by models and skills learned in, by, and for industrial corporations, if they were trained to manage at all. But we live and operate in a post-industrial, service-based economy. As we saw in Chapter 1, a service-based organization is radically different from an industrial corporation. To be successful, it needs a service culture, service management, and service-driven employees. All of this can come through carefully developed, easily understood, and accepted training.

Now let's examine the type of training that develops customer contact people.

According to some authorities in the field of service management, the people who contact your customers are the most important people in your organization. As Jan Carlzon says, "If you're not serving the customer, you'd better be serving someone who is."[7]

Recall our earlier discussion of cycles of service and the points of contact with customers (see Chapter 10). In this contact, the customer is forming an impression of your organization—good or bad. Which means that your customers' impressions of your organization are made almost solely by how your contact people treat them. As a result, from the customer's view, contact people are the single most important group in your organization.

According to highly profitable companies like Dana, Wal-Mart, and Scandinavian Airlines, an organization's chart therefore should look like Figure 13-1:[8]

This may seem extreme, but the plain fact is that your CSRs can do your organization the most good of anyone in the organization. If they are unhappy, untrained, or both, they can do the most harm.

Selecting CRSs

Customer-contact employees are the backbone of the service delivery system. They have an immediate and uncensored impact upon customers. In selecting frontline employees, look for more than just experience or skills. Look for the attitudes, aptitude, and characteristics that increase success in these all-important customer contact positions. This dictates careful screening and selection—above and beyond your normal personnel selection procedures.

A standard test helps. Fortunately, personnel selection is one of the many areas that has benefited from automation.

The rationale behind high-tech personnel selection is that most hirers base their decisions on hunches and barebones data, such as application forms and references. But research has found that:

• Sixty percent of resumes contain false data.
• Most references give only positive information.
• Interviewing tells you only how candidates look and how they perform in interviews.

A new scientific hiring method, a computerized aptitude survey, provides a high-tech way to hire the best people. It works like this:

1. Researchers determine what qualities make up a desirable customer-contact person. By talking to managers and by observing those CSRs you designate as your best, they draw up a customized profile to fit your organization.

Figure 13-1.   Revised chart.

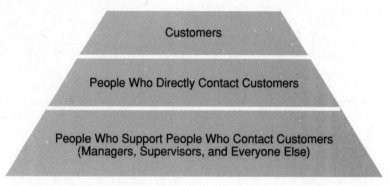

Reprinted by courtesy of Learning Dynamics, Inc.

2. They then select standardized tests that will measure the behaviors they've identified as most important to success in your industry.
3. Next they validate the test by giving it to the CSRs you've identified as your best.
4. They select those items on which your best people scored well and combine them into a customized test for you.

If you don't want to take the time to have a customized profile drawn up, you can also use their database of successful CSRs in your industry. So far, extensive data exist on such jobs as reservations agents, telephone collectors, and pest control technicians.[9]

If this seems like too much trouble, consider IBM's hiring process. When IBM hires someone at, say, a $20,000 starting salary, it doesn't look at its expenses as just the salary, fringes, and time spent hiring. IBM expects new hires to spend the rest of their career there, and figures it's going to spend $1 million over the course of the employee's career lifetime. So one way to focus on selection is to look at each new position as a $1 million investment.

Companies That Win With Service

The effectiveness of a multi-level training approach has been proven again and again by some of the world's outstanding success stories.

McDonald's emphasizes the benefits of customer service to its employees this way:[10]

- You will learn important skills, and they will help you succeed in life, regardless of whatever you choose to do after you work here.
- You will get the satisfaction of knowing that your work helps others—customers and fellow workers—as well as yourself.
- You will learn how to motivate customers and fellow employees. This helps you get what you want from life.
- You will discover things about yourself and your abilities that you did not realize.
- You will learn how an effective system works.
- If you do well, customers will come back. The better you do, the better the organization does, and the better for the whole economy.

Southland Corporation demonstrated dramatically the value of good service. It identified top service in their 7-Eleven stores through written tests and mystery shoppers. Their best service people shared over $3 million in cash and prizes.[11]

Here is what has happened in just a few companies.

The Marriott Corporation believes firmly in the impact of training on the bottom line. As Chairman Willard Marriott says, "We are in the people business. From waiters to maids to truck drivers, our employees must be able to get along pleasantly with others all day long." His 140,000 employees make 6 million customer contacts a day. Marriott spends over $20 million a year on training.

British Airways put all 37,000 of its employees through a two-day customer service seminar in its attempt to become the best airline in the world. Passengers note, "The customer-first program has unquestionably produced some strong and visible signs of a new day for BA. We have seen a marked change in the quality of interpersonal attention—warmth, friendliness, attentiveness. . . ."

Although no figures are available, Walt Disney Productions' commitment to customers and to training is legendary. For example, ticket-takers are given four thirteen-hour days of instruction before they go "on stage" in this seemingly mundane job. New hires learn about Guests—not lower-case "c" customers but upper-case "G" Guests.

Why does it take four days to learn how to take tickets? Disney's response: What happens if someone wants to know where the restrooms are, when the parade starts, what bus to take to get back to the campgrounds? Cast Members need to know the answers and where to get the answers quickly. After all, they are on stage and help produce the Show for the Guests.

Their job is "to help guests enjoy the party."

C&P Telephone

Probably the most dramatic—and sensible—career development and retainment example we've been involved with is the work at C&P Telephone in Washington, D.C., initiated by Glenn Evans.

As a support staff supervisor (since promoted to manager of customer service operations), Evans was confronted with a Catch-22 dilemma.

The company's restructuring was creating a "window of opportunity" for first-level managers, and C&P was committed to promoting from within. But for candidates to move into the managerial ranks, each one had to successfully complete the company's Management Assessment Center program.

And therein was the problem. Although the manager-candidates were motivated to move ahead, their rate of failure at the assessment center was disheartening. Most simply couldn't pass, leaving Evans fuming in frustration, "Why can't we get our people through?"

He had been through the program himself and had scored in the highest category. And, in Evans's words, he'd had no "special aptitude or experience in management." But, he reasoned, the candidates he was seeing had never worked around managers or seen the behavior that managers used on the job. His candidates came "right off the poles."

Evans hit upon the idea of introductory training—not to prepare candidates for the tests but to help them understand the manager's role and to pinpoint their strengths, weaknesses, and areas for further study.

He took one of Learning Dynamics' generic training programs, "tinkered with the content," and then did a pilot program. The successful completion rate of manager-candidates skyrocketed to 75 percent, many times better than the previous completion rate.

More important than percentage increases, however, Evans's program is developing a pool of potential management employees for future company needs—a significant step in the dramatic growth that all C&P Telephone executives anticipate.

People who have managed both service firms and manufacturing firms say a major difference between the two types of companies is the difficulty of achieving consistently high quality in service. Controlling high quality is particularly difficult for services with a high level of direct public contact. Yet those companies that have achieved consistent quality often create services that are very profitable, with a highly loyal customer base. Marriott Hotels has discovered many things about achieving service excellence that escape its competitors. For example:

- One of the most effective forms of quality control is to tap employees' inner desire to provide good service—as opposed to merely throwing more supervision at a problem.
- Service goals almost without fail are meaningful to down-the-line employees.

A sense of personal accountability is crucial. You know you have achieved it when a first-line worker says, "Each one of us *is* the company."

How do you train people to feel this way? The Marriott Corporation pays particular attention to employee training, involvement, incentives, and, in some cases, ownership.

In addition, management is on a first-name basis. Their ads feature employees. Internal communications all convey the company's purpose and standards. As Willard Marriott put it, "You can't make happy guests with unhappy employees."

Unfortunately, you can't train people to "have a good attitude," because you can't measure a "good attitude." However, you can train people to perform specific, customer-friendly behaviors and then measure their performance and your success factors: customer ratings, repeat business, market share, morale, and turnover. By these results, you'll know whether your employees have customer-friendly attitudes or not.

Earlier we discussed the importance of having everyone in the organization receive training. And when it comes to training contact people, everybody plays a part in employee education.

Senior executives commit the resources, model service-driven, customer-friendly behaviors, and provide rewards for the rest of the organization.

Managers and supervisors also act as role models and serve as resources, coaches, and reinforcers for the training. In some organizations, they may conduct the training.

The more confident contact people feel, the better they'll serve the customer. As Albrecht and Zemke say: "Helping people review their personal effectiveness and rekindle their energies will automatically pay off on the job. . . . Persons who feel better about themselves, and who have a clearer perspective on life goals, personal skills, and rewards, will have more creative energy to put into the job." [12]

Notes

1. Warren Blanding, Leslie Hansen Harps, and William R. Henry, Jr., *133 Ways to Handle Customer Complaints* (Silver Spring, Md.: Marketing Publications Inc., 1979), p. 8.

2. TARP (Technical Assistance Research Programs Institute), "Consumer Complaint Handling in America: An Update Study" (Washington, D.C.: U.S. Office of Consumer Affairs, 1986).

3. Rosabeth Moss Kanter, "The Middle Manager as Innovator," *Harvard Business Review*, Reprint No. 82407.

4. *Ibid.*

5. Ed Tharp, "Redefining Quality in an Industry in Transition," in Jay Sprechler, *When America Does It Right* (Norcross, Ga.: Industrial Engineering and Management Press, 1988), p. 570.

6. James E. Stutz, "Service Quality and Shareholder Value," in Sprechler, *When America Does It Right*, pp. 475–476.

7. Karl Albrecht and Ron Zemke, *Service America* (Homewood, Ill.: Dow Jones-Irwin, 1985).

8. Tom Peters and Nancy Austin, *A Passion for Excellence* (New York: Random House, 1985), p. 318.

9. Robert Berk, "The Telephone Collector Aptitude Survey," Personnel Strategy Consultants.

10. Robert Desatnick, *Managing to Keep the Customer* (San Francisco: Jossey-Bass, 1981), p. 35.

11. "Thanks a Million," public relations package from 7-Eleven, February 1987.

12. Albrecht and Zemke, *Service America*.

Fourteen

Step 9: Empowering Employees to Solve and Prevent Problems

An important part of driving your organization for customers is empowering employees with the responsibility and authority to meet customers' needs and expectations. In this chapter we'll look at this process in detail.

The Goals of Empowerment

The most difficult part of moving an organization from a customer-indifferent to a customer-driven culture is solving the problems customers are experiencing now. Empowerment simplifies and accelerates the problem-solving process and focuses employees on preventing future problems, while continuously improving service quality from the customer's perspective.

The principle behind empowerment is to push decision-making and complaint-resolution down to the lowest possible level. You empower the people who are dealing with customers to make decisions in customers' behalf and to solve their problems on the spot, if at all possible. In addition, you gain the participation and the input of the people who know your customers best and focus them on solving problems, rather than refer customers to superiors or dismiss them with "That's-company-policy" replies.

Some companies do leave customer satisfaction to the discretion of their CSRs. Often, however, such a policy can lead to chaos. We prefer a system that trains people in problem-solving skills through a network of departmental or cross-functional groups led by internal leaders. This system includes built-in measurements, so it is easily controlled. Furthermore, it is easy and fun.

The network process trains people at all levels in powerful, decep-

173

tively simple skills to make your customers happy. At the same time, empowering staff via these skills increases your employees' value and builds their self-esteem.

To create a customer-driven environment, you need customer feedback at every step of the process. Most organizational problems are solved in a vacuum, considering only the company's needs. This approach can result in little or no positive change for customers. When customers are part of the process, however, you help assure their buy-in to the solution.

You begin, of course, by solving present customers' problems. But your long-term goal is continuous improvement. Your employees progress from problem solving to problem prevention to continuous, customer-driven improvement. This ongoing, pro-active approach gives your company a clear advantage over companies that solve problems only after they develop.

Also, by solving problems' root causes instead of continuously fighting fires, you cut costs of mistakes, wasted resources, customer dissatisfaction, and poor word-of-mouth. All of these factors lose customers and reduce profits.

We base our approach to customer-driven problem solving on the following beliefs:[1]

1. A "problem" exists only if it affects a customer.
2. Working in a group usually improves the problem-solving process by cross-fertilizing and hitchhiking on each others' ideas. Teams can create solutions faster than most individuals can working alone.
3. The first step in problem solving is becoming aware of the problem. Recognizing the situation as it is begins the means to a solution.
4. Problems have many causes; situations exist because a number of forces push them that way. Identifying the forces may give you a direction for changing the situation.
5. Effective decisions depend on accurate information and on generating new ways of solving problems.
6. Everyone is creative. You only need to learn how to tap your creative center.
7. To be more creative, you simply look at the same things as everyone else and then *think something different.*
8. Problem solvers are free to contribute their best efforts, break rules, stop being practical, make mistakes, look into outside areas, and have fun—without penalty.
9. "Solving" a problem isn't worth much unless you can implement

your decision. So you need to be sensitive to the needs of the people who will carry out the solution.

10. The main objective in this process is to prevent problems and continuously improve. Solving problems is only one step toward this goal.

Rational vs. Creative Problem Solving

You can solve problems through rational (analytical) methods, such as flowcharts and fishbones or force-field analysis, and/or through creative methods, such as brainstorming, "What If," and challenging the rules (all discussed in this chapter), or through a combination of these methods.

To see how you do at solving problems using these different approaches, read the "Positions Problem" in Worksheet 30, giving yourself ten minutes to come up with the answer.[2]

Now try the "Warehouse Problem" in Worksheet 31. Again give yourself ten minutes to find a solution.[3]

Idea

Now let's look at a new way to combine rational and creative problem-solving skills to solve customer problems.

This is a four-step process called IDEA (for "Identify, Diagnose, Explore, and Act").

1. *Identify the problem.* What hurts? Where does it hurt? How much does it hurt?
2. *Diagnose for root causes.* Use a scientific or rational approach.
3. *Explore solution.* Use creative problem-solving approaches.
4. *Act on the solution.*

This process focuses employees on customer needs and customer satisfaction, because, as we've said repeatedly, customer satisfaction is not a product that you can see, taste, try on, or test drive; it is in the head of each customer.

We need to see service as a way to understand and meet customers' needs and expectations. Problems exist when there are large gaps between what our customers want and what we deliver. Therefore, to identify a customer service problem, the very best place to start is, of course, with your customers. Ask them what their ideal service would be. How close or far away are you to this ideal? The gap between the customer's

(text continues on page 177)

Worksheet 30. Positions Problem

One department of a large company consists of a clerk, word processor, customer service rep (CSR), salesperson, and manager. Betty Sevald, Tom Arnold, Ed Hurlbert, Sidney Cross, and Ted Tucker work in the department, but not necessarily in that order.

Can you determine who holds what position, based on the following data?

1. The word processor (WP) bandaged the manager's finger when he cut it.
2. While the CSR and manager were out of town, the salesperson took Tucker and Cross to lunch.
3. The salesperson is a fine bridge player, and Arnold admires his ability.
4. Tucker invited the word processor out to dinner, but his invitation was not accepted.

This is analytical problem solving: There is only one right answer, reached by deductive reasoning. You're best off using a model such as a grid or matrix like this one:

Name	Manager	CSE	Clerk	WP	Sales
Betty					
Tom					
Ed					
Sidney					
Ted					

Answers:

1. The manager is male (clue 1), so it's not Betty.
2. Sidney and Ted can't be CSR, salesperson, or manager (clue 2). So they must be WP and clerk.
3. Salesperson is a male, so it can't be Betty, and it can't be Tom, so it must be Ed. This means Tom must be the manager, and Betty must be the CSR.
4. Ted isn't the word processor (clues 2 and 4), so he must be the clerk, and that leaves Sidney as the word processor (clue 2).

Worksheet 31. Warehouse Problem

One day my boss ordered me to take a quick inventory of our warehouse. The warehouse held several thousand buckets, all stacked the same height. If the stacks had been in regular rows, the task would have been fairly simple. Unfortunately, the stacks were pushed together in an irregular mess.

It was impossible to walk over the buckets to count the stacks, and there was not enough time to straighten them up for counting; the warehouse was closing in half an hour.

How could I count the buckets in less than half an hour without touching a single bucket?_____

_____

_____

This is "creative" problem solving. It requires:

• Drawing on experience
• Breaking problems down in various ways
• Thinking up as many solutions as possible
• Combining ideas and trying them out to see what works

There are usually several possible answers to creative problems.

One Possible Answer:

Count the number of buckets in one stack, get above the buckets, take photos of the tops of the stacks with an instant camera, count the top buckets in the pictures, and multiply by the number in each stack.

ideal and your delivery are essentially the problems or potential problems.

Identifying the Problem: Gap Analysis

To learn the gaps between what you do and what your customers expect, begin by examining what you do from your customers' (internal or external) point of view. Then complete the Customer Expectations Form, following the directions in Worksheet 32:

Next study the areas your customers rated 3 (very important) in the second column, 2 (meets expectations adequately), or 1 (does not meet expectations) in the third column. These are your "gaps."

(text continues on page 179)

Worksheet 32. Gap Analysis

To determine the gaps between what you do and what your customers expect, complete the following analysis:

1. Fill in your four most important outputs (products or services) in the space indicated.

2. Visit or talk with at least three customers to determine what they expect for each of your listed product or service outputs, how important each expectation is, and how the customers rate your company in providing it.

3. Fill in what you learn about your customers and their expectations for each product or service you've listed.

4. Note how important each expectation is to the customer on the following scale:

$$1 = \text{Unimportant/unnecessary}$$
$$2 = \text{Somewhat important}$$
$$3 = \text{Very important}$$

5. Indicate how your customers rate your product or service in this area on the following scale:

$$1 = \text{Does not meet expectations}$$
$$2 = \text{Meets expectations adequately}$$
$$3 = \text{Superior (exceeds expectations)}$$

6. List also any problems you uncover that you didn't know about.

a. Product/Service _____

Expectations	Importance	Rating
_____	_____	_____
_____	_____	_____
_____	_____	_____

b. Product/Service _____

Expectations	Importance	Rating
_____	_____	_____
_____	_____	_____

c. Product/Service _____

Expectations	Importance	Rating
_____	_____	_____
_____	_____	_____
_____	_____	_____

d. Product/Service _____

Expectations	Importance	Rating
_____	_____	_____
_____	_____	_____
_____	_____	_____

e. Problems Learned

_____

_____

Reprinted by courtesy of Learning Dynamics, Inc.

List these gaps in Worksheet 33. Then rate their priority to your team, to your organization, or to you on a scale of 1 (low) to 10 (high).

Studying the gaps between what you provide and what your customers need will give you critical feedback on the source of your problems and on what your customers need and expect.

Another way to identify problems is to ask "Is/Is Not" questions that specify the identity, location, timing, and extent of the deviation.[4] These questions include:

- *Who* is involved?
- *What* is the deviation? What is it not? (Sometimes it helps to pinpoint what it is by specifying other difficulties you might expect but are not having.)
- *Where* is it? (Exactly where did it happen—what part of the store or branch? Again, where would you normally expect this kind of problem to occur, but it didn't?)
- *When* did it occur? What was the precise time, date, season?
- *How* extensive? How big is the problem? How often does it occur? What is the trend?

Worksheet 33. Evaluate the Gaps

Study the gaps between what you provide and what your customers need. Then rate their priority.

Directions:

1. Note areas that your customers rated important and in which your performance is not superior. Pay particular attention to ratings of 3 (Very Important) in the second column and 2 (Meets expectations adequately) or 1 (Does not meet expectations) in the third column. These are your "gaps."
2. Study each of these gaps and, on a scale of 1 (least important) to 10 (most), rate its priority to you, your team, and your organization.

Gap	*Priority*
_____	_____
_____	_____
_____	_____
_____	_____
_____	_____
_____	_____
_____	_____
_____	_____

Reprinted by courtesy of Learning Dynamics, Inc.

Answering these questions will help you pinpoint what is relevant and what is not.

Disputes often arise over the accuracy of information. So, while you are in the process, separate and categorize information into Fact, Assumption, and Inference.

A *fact* is something that has actually happened or is known to be true. An *assumption* is a guess at a fact. An *inference* is a judgment made by reasoning from known or implied facts.

Your ultimate objective in tightly specifying the gap is to learn what is distinctive about the relevant facts: The distinctions will often point to the cause. Once you know the cause, you can work toward a solution.

To see how this works in practice, try Worksheet 34.

(*text continues on page 185*)

Worksheet 34. Specifying the Gap

For the past two weeks, the number of complaints about merchandise returns not being credited to accounts has increased from two to five a day. It's happened at all our stores. Investigation shows this problem occurs almost totally with new hires. This is particularly puzzling, since we beefed up our cash register training a month ago.

Step 1. *Answer the "Is/Is Not" questions to define what the problem is.*

Question	Is	Is Not
Who		
What		
Where		
When		
Extent		

(continues)

Worksheet 34 (continued)

Suggested Answers

Question	Is	Is Not
Who	New workers	Experienced ones
What	Customer complaints	Customer complaints
	about credits	about charges
Where	All stores	One store
	One region	
When	Two weeks ago	Constantly
Extent	Five a day. Has major	Previous average of two
	and negative impact	a day
	on customers' image	
	of us	

Step 2. *Determine the most likely cause(s).* Reexamine the problem itself and list what is distinctive about the conditions and facts specified by your Is/Is Not questions. In addition, seek out possible changes and relevant facts that might impact on the problem. Finally, try to establish relationships—correlate the various pieces of information that might tie together.

Our point is: There is something distinctive about every set of relevant facts, and your objective is to pinpoint what change (or changes) might be causing that distinction.

Let's examine our case to see what clues we can come up with to help us pinpoint the change that might be causing the problem behavior.

Look for distinctions and changes that explain the differences between the Is and Is Not columns.

Distinctions

_____

_____

_____

What can we identify in the way of Is/Is Not distinctions?
a. It involves new employees, not old ones.
b. It involves credits, not charges.
c. It started two weeks ago.

What else has changed?
"We enhanced our cash register training."

Now we have four clues. If we've done our research and analysis properly, the "most likely" cause of the problem should pop out at us. If not, we'll have to reexamine all the critical clues—the relevant facts, distinctions, and changes—to see what's missing. We may have to go back and do some additional probing or questioning for important information that was overlooked or not readily available. The "most likely" cause, in many instances, is the one that explains all the facts in our specification of the Is/Is Not boxes.

Now you can determine the possible causes. Test each one to see if it meets the Is/Is Not specifications. Then choose the most likely cause (Steps 3 and 4).

Step 3. *Generate possible causes, and see if each one explains the distinctions noted in Step 2.*

Possible Causes	*Test*
_____	_____
_____	_____
	_____
	_____
_____	_____
_____	_____
	_____

(*continues*)

Worksheet 34 (*continued*)

Possible Causes	*Test*
_____	_____
_____	_____
_____	_____
_____	_____
_____	_____
_____	_____
_____	_____
_____	_____

Step 4. Choose the most likely explanation. Then talk to the people involved to see how they feel and move to Problem Solving.

Suggested Answers

Possible Causes	Test
New bunch of employees incompetent	Then why do they handle charges okay?
Bookkeeping department is too slow to credit	Then why only with new cash register employees?
"Enhanced" training program defective	Checks out. Time training was changed coincides with when new hires began making credits that now don't show up on statements.

Figure 14-1. Root cause analysis.
To depict graphically the causes of a problem, draw a chart like the following "fishbone." Put the problem on the right side, or fish's head. Write the main factors which contribute to the effect at the ends of the "bones."

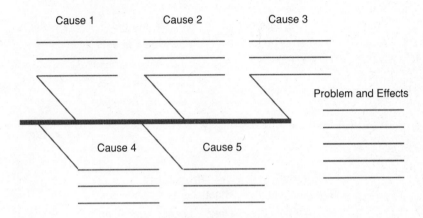

Reprinted by courtesy of Learning Dynamics, Inc.

Diagnosing the Problem

There are many ways of identifying and diagnosing problems. The method you use depends a great deal on your situation and the kinds of problems you are facing. Let's examine a few of the classic ways of diagnosing the significant root causes of a problem.

Fishbone Analysis

In Fishbone Analysis, you chart the problem to see if you can determine the root cause of why you're not meeting the needs of your customers as well as you would like. (It's called fishbone because that is what the diagram resembles. See Figure 14-1.)

To do a Fishbone Analysis, draw a chart like the one in Figure 14-1 and put the problem on the right side, or at the fish's head. Write the main factors which contribute to the effect at the ends of the "bones."

If it's a technical problem, you can subgroup the main factors under the headings, "Human," "Machine," "Materials," "Method," and "Environment." If it's a sales problem, use the factors, "People," "Product," "Price," and "Promotion."

On each of the bones, fill in the specific factors that you consider causes. Collect data to see how important each of the causes is.

Figure 14-2.   Exercise: Fishbone Diagram.
An airline analyzing the cause of late departures started with five possible causes: material, personnel, procedure, equipment, and other. The list looked like this:

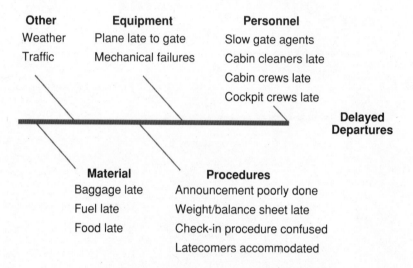

Reprinted by courtesy of Learning Dynamics, Inc.

For example, Midway Airlines determined that a prime concern of business customers was on-time arrivals. Traditionally, airlines consider any flight operating within fifteen minutes of schedule "on time." But Midway realized that this was not good enough, so it made its standard five minutes.[5]

The company used a fishbone analysis to pinpoint the cause of so many late departures. They started with five possible causes: material, personnel, procedure, equipment, and other.

Midway employees had a pretty good idea of what was causing the delays. Their suggestions are charted in Figure 14-2.

The airline collected statistics on these causes and found the following:

Cause	Percentage
Late passengers	53%
Waiting for pushback	15
Waiting for fueling	11

Late weight and balance sheet   9

All other   12

Just four causes accounted for 88 percent of the delays. The chief cause (as many contact people felt) was accommodating late passengers—not passengers late because of connecting flights but passengers who got to the airport late.

Individual gate agents had been so anxious for Midway not to lose fares that they let late passengers on board, forgetting the annoyance to passengers who arrived on time.

Midway established a policy of operating on time and giving top service to passengers who were ready to fly on schedule. As a result, the number of passengers getting to the airport late declined. (The delays in "pushback"—moving the aircraft away from the gate with motorized tugs—were reduced by better scheduling of tugs in some locations and by working more closely with subcontractors in other locations. Management also worked with fuel suppliers to improve their performance.)

Pareto Analyses

In many cases, it turns out that 20 percent of the factors cause 80 percent of the problems. For example, 20 percent of the customers account for 80 percent of overdue bills. Pareto Analyses, named for a nineteenth-century economist, highlight the few major causes.

In a Pareto Analysis, you gather data on each cause (perhaps those suggested by a Fishbone Analysis) and display them in descending order. We've done this on American League baseball Most Valuable Players in Figure 14-3.

By looking at the causes, from the biggest to the smallest, you are able to concentrate your resources where they will do the most good.

Suppose human factors account for 60 percent of the causes, materials 25 percent, method 12 percent, and other 3 percent. You would concentrate your problem solving on interpersonal causes first and material causes second.

Force-Field Analysis

Force-Field Analysis is based on the theory that in any problem, there are forces supporting and opposing change. If you can strengthen the forces supporting change and/or weaken those opposing it, you'll move from the status quo to the desired state.[6]

To do a Force-Field Analysis, you write the current situation on the left side of a chart and the desired situation on the right (see Figure 14-

Figure 14-3. Pareto chart.

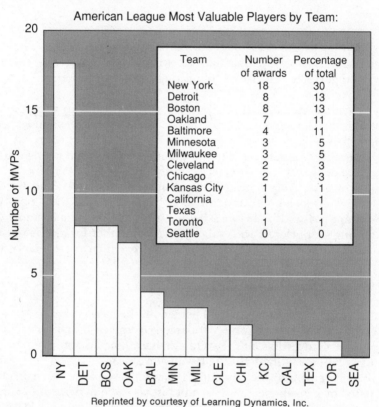

American League Most Valuable Players by Team:

Team	Number of awards	Percentage of total
New York	18	30
Detroit	8	13
Boston	8	13
Oakland	7	11
Baltimore	4	11
Minnesota	3	5
Milwaukee	3	5
Cleveland	2	3
Chicago	2	3
Kansas City	1	1
California	1	1
Texas	1	1
Toronto	1	1
Seattle	0	0

Reprinted by courtesy of Learning Dynamics, Inc.

4). Put supporting forces (those pushing toward the desired situation) on the left and opposing forces (those resisting the desired situation) on the right. (For example, one manager wanted to improve service but found it was not easy. He identified his "forces" as shown in Figure 14-5.) Finally you rate each force on a scale of 1 (very weak) to 5 (very strong). Now you need to determine how to strengthen the supporting forces and weaken the opposing ones.

Exploring Solutions: Techniques for Creative Thinking

When you've identified and diagnosed the problem, you'll know its cost in dollars, time, lost customers, and other areas.

Figure 14-4.   Force-Field Analysis.

Directions: Analyze the forces promoting and opposing change.

Current Situation: _____   Desired Situation: _____

Supporting Forces   Opposing Forces

_____   _____

_____   _____

_____   _____

_____   _____

_____   _____

_____   _____

_____   _____

_____   _____

_____   _____

_____   _____

_____   _____

Reprinted by courtesy of Learning Dynamics, Inc.

Now put your data aside for a while, and explore solutions with some creative techniques. Later on you can be practical. For now, just try to sprout new ideas.

Let's try it out. Look at the diagram in Figure 14-6. What is it?*

To trigger creative thinking, brainstorm (in writing or in a group) your ideas of what the illustration in Figure 14-6 is.

Having trouble? Try these idea triggers:

*From a course given by Jeanne Millson, "Applied Imagination," Cambridge, Massachusetts, 1988.

Figure 14-5.   Force-Field Analysis example.

Current Situation: <u>Our accuracy</u>   Desired Situation: <u>We want to</u>

<u>is only adequate.</u>   <u>exceed customers' expectations.</u>

       Supporting Forces   Opposing Forces

1. Some of our competitors are   1. Most competitors are worse.
   better.

2. When we goof, we get   2. We don't get many complaints.
   vociferous complaints.

3. We want to increase market   3. We've done it this way a long
   share.   time.

4. Our employees want to do   4. Top management thinks we're
   better.   good enough.

5. Increased accuracy would   5. Corporate culture is "don't rock
   be inexpensive.   the boat."

Reprinted by courtesy of Learning Dynamics, Inc.

- Substitute: What could it be used for instead of something else?
- Combine: What could it be combined with?
- Adapt: What could it be adapted to?
- Magnify: What if it were huge?
- Reduce: What if it were tiny?
- Reverse: Turn it upside down.
- Rearrange: Suppose you change the order.
- Change perspective: See it from earth, in the sky; visualize it from outer space; get under, on top of, or behind it.

Some ideas: a bird with an egg; the letters "YOY" with tails; chopsticks with a wonton; footprints on Mars; an addition to Stonehenge; two sperm vying for an egg; a sleeping-bag hammock; an oversized soccer

Figure 14-6.   First brainstorming exercise: What is it?

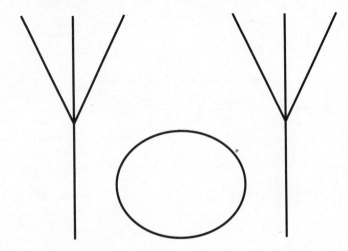

game; an unsuccessful optical illusion; a build-it-yourself face; a bag of leaves between two naked trees; or a water ballet.

Brainstorming

What does this silly exercise have to do with problem solving? It illustrates that you really do have a creative center—a powerful resource for solutions to problems. This leads us to brainstorming, a classic means to tap the creativity of a group—to get as many ideas as possible.

There are five rules for brainstorming:

1. All ideas, no matter how wild, are welcome.
2. No criticism is allowed.
3. Hitchhike; that is, use others' ideas as a jumping-off point for your own.
4. Freewheel—go with your thought.
5. Be outrageous. It is completely acceptable.

Now try a brainstorming exercise:

1. Select a problem you face now, or use the following problem: How to be sure customer service representatives (or other contact people) display a "good attitude."
2. Brainstorm ideas in your group, according to the rules above.
3. When you are finished generating and listing ideas, look over the list and refine or fine-tune ideas.

Idea	Refinement
_____	_____
_____	_____
_____	_____
_____	_____
_____	_____
_____	_____
_____	_____
_____	_____
_____	_____
_____	_____
_____	_____
_____	_____
_____	_____
_____	_____

Phases of Brainstorming

The process of brainstorming has two distinct phases.

1. *Idea Generation.* Everyone takes turns contributing as many ideas as possible. No "criticism" means group members avoid phrases like:

- "We've tried it before."
- "That's not practical."

- "It's not in the budget."
- "People aren't ready for it."
- "Other departments won't stand for it."
- "Customers won't accept it."
- "It violates policy."
- "The time isn't right to make changes."
- "Nobody's ever tried it."
- "That's not the way everybody else does it."
- "It'll take too long (or too much work)."

Try the idea triggers from the previous exercise, i.e., change perspective; make objects larger or smaller; substitute or eliminate a part; look at it from outer space.

2. *Idea Refinement.* When you're finished listing ideas, try to find something useful in each.

There are times when you can stimulate your imagination by asking yourself questions such as "What's going on?" "What does that mean?" "How else can I interpret it?" These are special questions, the kind you ask when you're looking for new ideas.

There's another "what is it" drawing in Figure 14-7.[7] Use brainstorming to identify it.

If you look at it one way, it's a bird. If you look at it another way, it could be a question mark. If you turn it upside down, it looks like a seal juggling a ball on its nose. By continued questioning and not deciding, you generate a variety of ideas.

The key point: don't decide that there is only one "right" answer or one way to do things. Try looking at things ambiguously. Children have the ability to do this. And so do you, if you've ever used a brick as a door stop, made chimes out of forks and spoons, or used a ballpoint pen as a hole punch.

The ability to keep questioning is an important part of creative thinking.

Challenging the Rules

"Challenging the Rules" is another technique for creative problem solving.[8]

Creative thinking involves playing with what you know, and this may mean breaking out of one pattern in order to create a new one. Thus one effective creative thinking strategy is to challenge the existing rules.

Copernicus broke the rule that stated that the earth is the center of the universe.

Napoleon broke the rules on the proper way to wage war.

Figure 14-7.   Second brainstorming exercise: What is it?

Reprinted from Roger van Oech, *A Whack on the Side of the Head: How to Unlock Your Mind for Innovation* (New York: Warner Books, 1988), page 8.

Beethoven broke the rules on how a symphony should be written.

Think about it: almost every advance in art, science, technology, business, marketing, cooking, medicine, agriculture, and design has occurred when someone challenged the rules and tried another approach.

"What-If" Techniques

Another creative problem-solving technique, called "What If," draws on our ability to imagine situations that don't exist at present. This ability empowers our thinking in two major ways.[9]

First, it enables us to anticipate the future. We're able to ask ourselves, "Suppose it rains tomorrow? What would happen to our picnic? What other arrangements can we make?" By simulating such possibilities mentally we can plan for the future.

Second, since our thinking is not bound by real-world constraints, we can generate ideas that are unrelated to experience. For example, imagine what would happen if gravity stopped for one second every day. What would things look like? What would land surfaces look like? How about the oceans and rivers? How would life have developed under such conditions? Would living things have special zero-gravity adaptive features? How would houses be designed? Imagine your living room. How would you design it and its furnishings if gravity stopped for one second every day?

You do "What If" when you dream or imagine anything that doesn't actually exist. And the results of such seemingly playful speculation need not be playful at all.

A noted scientist once asked himself, "What if I were falling through space in an elevator at the speed of light and there were a hole in the side of the elevator? What would happen?" By investigating the ramifications of such a possibility, Albert Einstein developed some of his early relativity concepts. The innovator is constantly challenging the rules. Most people will say, "As a rule, if you do XYZ, you will get ABC." "ABC" can be a marketing strategy, an engineering process, an accounting system, or a package design. The innovator will play with XYZ and look for results outside the usual rules and guidelines.

You did this in the exercise about gravity. Similarly, you can do it when you dream or imagine anything that doesn't actually exist.

Asking "What if?" is an easy way to get your imagination going. To do it, you simply ask "What if?" and then finish the question with some contrary-to-fact condition, idea or situation: What if———?

The what-if question can be whatever you wish, just as long as it is not a currently existing situation. The nice thing about "what-iffing" is that it allows you to suspend a few rules and assumptions and get into a creative frame of mind. Here are a few examples to play with on a rainy Sunday:

- What if animals became more intelligent than people?
- What if human life expectancy were 200 years?
- What if somebody developed bacteria that produced petroleum?
- What if there became two of you when you looked in the mirror?
- What if everybody in your company played a musical instrument, and you had a concert every Friday afternoon at 3:00?
- What if people didn't need to sleep?

Just asking the what-if question is not only a lot of fun, it also gives you the freedom to think something different.

Analyzing Benefits

Now it is decision time. If you are still wavering, list two or three possible solutions. Then, in Worksheet 35, list the benefits of each proposed solution. Rate those benefits according to the 0 to 3 scale and add up the total for each solution. Now choose the best solution, based on all you've done so far.

As a final step, talk to some customers and test out your proposed solution. Listen carefully to their reaction and to their suggestions for improving or changing your solution. Check out the cost and benefits of customers' ideas, if any. And do take their ideas seriously. Remember, over 80 percent of new product/service ideas come from customers.

Worksheet 35. Analyzing Benefits

Choose the best solution based on what you've done so far:

1. List possible ideas for a solution below.
2. List the benefits that each solution would bring.
3. Rate those benefits according to the following scale:

   3—The solution must have this element.
   2—This element is important or critical to the solution, but we could live without it if everything else is in place.
   1—This element would be nice to have, but it isn't essential.
   0—This is really irrelevant.

4. Add up the total for each solution.

Possible Solution	Benefits	Rating
	Total	
	Total	
	Total	
Choice		

Reprinted by courtesy of Learning Dynamics, Inc.

Acting on the Solution

In the final stage of the IDEA process, you act on your best solution. You determine potential problems and plan on ways to avoid them; do a test or trial run, wherever possible; build support for your plan; and install a system for measuring and tracking progress.

There are many ways to avoid encountering problems as you act on your decision.

Threat Analysis

Brainstorm a list of things that could go wrong with your plan. Rate how probable each event is on a ten-point scale on which "1" means very unlikely and "10" is very certain. Try to think of ways you can prevent these things from happening. If you can't prevent them, plan for how you will deal with them. If there are potentially damaging events that you don't know how to deal with, look at whether other solutions to your problem (second and third choices) might be better.

Trial Run

Another tactic to ensure a smooth changeover is to try out or *pilot* the new situation on a low-risk basis before rolling it out. Find an area where threat is low and the potential for improvement is high (that is, where things can't get much worse). If the trial solution fails, nothing terrible will happen; if you succeed, the results will be dramatic.

Building Support

To be successful, your solution requires two key factors: (1) acceptance from the people affected, and (2) high quality.[10]

These factors are not always equally important. Some decisions require the highest quality, regardless of how people feel about them. For example, if your solution involves your community's drinking water supply, you need the highest quality you can achieve, even if it's not popular with certain special interest groups.

With other solutions, it's more important to get people's acceptance. For example, if you're assigning overtime, you want a solution that people will accept, rather than the most "rational" one. The "second best" solution may be preferable if more people will accept it.

Tracking and Measurement

Once you have implemented your solution, you need to track its success. Further, you want to prevent the problem recurring. The key to achieving this is measurement.

What do you measure? Whatever shows the quantity and/or quality of the process. Here are some ideas:

- Average order amount
- Average annual purchases per customer
- Overdue accounts receivable
- Turnaround time

At this point, you need to define "success" precisely. Don't set your initial goals too high; you'll tend to get discouraged and give up. Use the "Swiss cheese" approach: Poke holes in the goal to break it up into smaller problems (shorter-term goals).

Then, depending on your project, track your data using checksheets. Put a system into place to produce progress reports and/or an impact analysis so you can help guarantee the new way of doing work.

Case Example: Tracking System

A company was concerned with its late deliveries. Possible causes of late deliveries were:

- Underestimating the time it took to produce the product
- Underestimating the time it took to ship the product
- Failure of suppliers to deliver materials on time
- Unexpected downtime on equipment
- Changed requirements of customers

After analyzing the data, costs, and benefits, the managers decided that the root cause most susceptible to change was "unexpected downtime on equipment." They began a program of preventive maintenance.

For their success measure, they used difference in number of days between promised delivery and actual delivery. After several weeks, they found the results described in Figure 14-8.

The new program clearly improved performance. However, making deliveries five days late was still too late for the company, so it needs to examine other causes to reduce the average days late to less than one (the goal).

Summary

In summary, empowerment means giving people the authority and re-sources to make more decisions. When you focus on customers for life,

Figure 14-8.   Case example: tracking system.

A company concerned with its late deliveries began a program of preventive maintenance.

Their results:

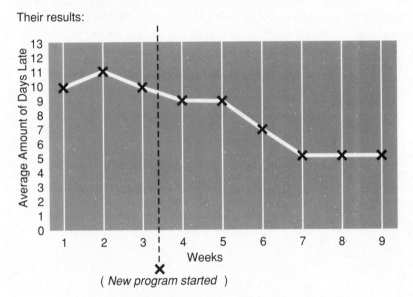

Reprinted by courtesy of Learning Dynamics, Inc.

you empower subordinates to solve more customer problems. But which decisions? And what kind of problems?

It depends on you, your company situation, and your degree of confidence in the people you empower. Some companies evaluate costs and benefits and set guidelines for people; *guidelines,* not hard-and-fast rules.

Is it worth it? Does it pay off?

Florida Power & Light Company is one organization that has trained its employees in problem-solving methods like these. Here are just some of the results:

• Employees discovered that 24 percent of their transformer outages were caused by wild animals. They suggested a "squirrel guard" to protect wires. The guard cost $3 and saved the company $150,000 a year.

• Another employee team found the company made about 60,000 billing errors yearly. The group recommended a self-monitoring system that cut errors to almost nothing.

• An employee-recommended change in the operation of soot blowers saved FPL $4.3 million in fuel expenses.

• Company cables running through poles were fraying too frequently. Employees suggested the poles' concrete holes be lined with Teflon, saving the company $150,000 a year.

• The Nuclear Regulatory Commission requires that a second copy of all quality assurance documents be kept in a remote file. Instead of having FPL store the duplicates, employees suggested the federal agency's own files serve as the backups. The NRC agreed, saving the company $100,000 a year.[11]

Overall savings amounted to $42 million a year—and a 26 percent reduction in customer complaints. Even if employees go wrong in solving some problems, it seems worthwhile when they achieve results like this.

Through a process of Identify-Diagnose-Explore-Act, your employees can solve and prevent problems. When they are trained and empowered as problem solvers, they will have a lot of information that is useful to you in your new roles. How to get that information from them—and how to give them the information they need to be effective—is the subject of our next chapter.

Notes

1. Dean Elias and Paul David, "A Guide to Problem Solving," in Leonard D. Goodstein and J. William Pfeiffer, eds., *The 1983 Annual for Facilitators, Trainers, and Consultants* (San Diego: University Associates, 1983), p. 150.
2. John E. Jones and J. William Pfeiffer, eds., *The 1981 Annual Handbook for Group Facilitators.* (San Diego: University Associates, 1981), p. 27.
3. *Ibid.*
4. C. H. Kepner and B. B. Tregoe, *Executive Problem Analysis and Decision Making.* (Princeton, N.J.: Princeton Research Press, 1973).
5. D. Dury Wyckoff, "New Tools for Achieving Service Quality," *The Cornell H.R.A. Quarterly,* November 1984, p. 80.
6. J. William Pfeiffer and John E. Jones, eds., *A Handbook of Structured Experiences for Human Relations Training.* (San Diego: University Associates, 1974), p. 79.
7. Roger von Oech, *A Whack on the Side of the Head: How to Unlock Your Mind for Innovation* (New York: Warner Books, 1988).
8. *Ibid.*
9. *Ibid.*
10. Rick Roskin, "Decision Style Inventory," in John E. Jones and J. William Pfeiffer, *The 1975 Annual Handbook for Group Facilitators* (San Diego: University Associates, 1975), p. 89.
11. "Florida Power & Light Company," American Productivity Center, Case Study 39, 1984.

Fifteen

Step 10: Communicating Feedback

The next step in the master strategy focuses on communication in your company.

Communication comes in two varieties:

1. Feedback you get *from* your employees
2. Feedback you give *to* your employees throughout the entire organization.

Through your internal communications system, you get information about customers' needs, wants, expectations, and problems; in addition, you "plug" the customer into the entire organization. At the same time, you meet your employees' needs for empowering information by transmitting company policy and procedures via the internal communications system.

A Lion in Your Office

How do you deal with the problems that customers report? As we discussed in Chapter 14, you start a network to deal with bad news. The aim of the network is to correct the customer's problem immediately. Later, you determine the cause of the problem, correct it, and establish the means to prevent its recurrence.

It's like finding a lion in your office.[1] Your first step is to get rid of the lion—"correct the situation immediately." Later, you'll try to find out how the lion got in there and how you can prevent it happening again.

This is not "problem solving," but "problem elimination."

The Problem-Solving Network

The principle behind the problem-solving network is to deal with problems at the lowest level possible. Thus, if front-line people or supervisors

Figure 15-1.   Problem report.

Your name: _____ Date: _____

Problem: _____

_____

_____

_____

- -

Action taken: _____

_____

_____

_____

Taken by: _____ Date: _____
Reprinted by courtesy of Learning Dynamics, Inc.

can solve a customer's problem, they do so. They then report the problem
and the solution on a problem report (see Figure 15-1). If the front-line
people can't deal with the problem, they report it to supervisors or network leaders on a problem report like the one in Figure 15-1.

This form may look like a traditional suggestion system, but it is not.
With a "suggestion box," you tell employees only if and when their suggestion is accepted. With the problem report, you take all reports seriously and give employees feedback on each problem they report.

The network works by (1) encouraging all employees to report problems about delivering quality service, and (2) publicizing the system (and
the rewards involved) so that everyone is aware of it.

If problems are beyond the abilities of the front-line employees or
their supervisors, a problem report goes to the network leader or to a
steering committee. They use clout to remove obstacles and provide solutions. They also decide when solutions should be shared with other
departments.

The key to a problem-solving network is to respond to all problems.
If a problem is serious enough for an employee to report, most of the
time it is serious enough to be solved, and in a timely manner. Quick
response shows employees you value them, and feedback like this is as
rewarding as praise.

An Early Warning System

Even though you've conducted your internal evaluation, you need to continue taking your customers' pulse on an ongoing basis. That's where your contact people come in.

They are the people in your organization closest to the customer. It's not always easy to get realistic feedback from subordinates, but if your environment encourages it, your people can be a gold mine of information.

The kind of information you want reported includes:

- What you're doing now that customers like
- What you're doing now that customers don't like
- What you're not doing now that customers would like you to do

Peters and Austin reviewed eighty studies of new product ideas in every kind of industry and concluded that "the great majority of ideas for new products come from the users . . . not just in high technology, but in the banking, health care and hamburger businesses."[2]

One-on-One Contact With Staff

Don't just rely on the formal system. Get out personally and talk to employees.

Ask your line people questions like, "What do we do to get in your way of delivering service quality? How can we ensure service excellence?"

Then do something about changing the things that line people say get in the way. Put up a scoreboard of the number of barriers removed. Enter the worst in a "Hall of Fame." Give a prize for the worst impediment that's reported each month.

Other Companies

Your contact people—and all of your employees—are also customers of other companies. In that capacity, they can report information on both competitors and potential customers.

As shoppers, they see what products are in the marketplace and what new products are needed. For example, a 3M employee noticed that his choir needed something to keep its performance notes in hymnals from flying away. Thus were Post-It note pads born.

As customers, contact people may use your products or services. They may even use your competitors'! They can tell you what they like or don't like about both.

Sales Force

Your customer service people aren't your only employees with extensive customer contact. Your salespeople have a great deal of contact, too. Use your salespeople as a source of feedback about what customers want, what they like about you, what the competition is offering, and how they feel about it.

Giving Feedback to Employees

One of the most important concepts presented by Blanchard and Johnson in their book *The One Minute Manager* is that people perform well when they feel good about themselves.[3] Although this idea is not new, the authors have expanded it into a creative technique that they call "one-minute praisings," an approach that gives managers an opportunity to reward their employees' desirable behaviors.

To use this approach, you make a conscious effort to notice subordinates doing things right. You may need to invest some time and energy in this effort, especially if some contact people are not performing well enough to get praised.

You also need to downplay negative behaviors. The rationale behind emphasizing positive behavior and deemphasizing negative is that you encourage positive behaviors.

Recall that the first law of human behavior states, "Behavior that is rewarded will be repeated." So you can give positive feedback (rewards) in numerous general areas:

- Exceeding performance standards
- Meeting standards consistently
- Staying calm with a difficult customer
- Going out of one's way to add value
- Any improvement, no matter how small

Feedback is most constructive when it follows these guidelines:[4]

1. It is specific rather than general.
   General: You're very friendly.
   Specific: I like the cheerful "hello" you give all your customers.
2. It immediately follows behavior.
   Delayed: Last month you made several errors.
   Immediate: There is an error on this form you just gave me.
3. It focuses on behavior people can control and avoids characteristics people cannot change, like size and age.

Avoid: Some customers don't want to talk to females.
Controllable: I'd like you to be more assertive in offering to help customers.
4. It avoids using the word "but." When giving feedback, "but" can be a put-down word. Some managers think they should balance criticism with praise. That's all right. The problem is that when you link praise and criticism in the same sentence with "but," your criticism cancels out your praise. So try using "and" instead of "but."
Negative: You handled that customer pretty well, but you kept her on hold too long.
Positive: You handled that customer pretty well. And next time, try calling back instead of putting her on hold for so long.

Of course, there is more to giving feedback to employees than your praise and/or criticism. They also need feedback in the form of customer information:

- Highlights of your market research
- Letters of praise and complaint
- Summaries of problems that were solved
- Sales and market share results
- Samples of phone calls
- Mystery shopper reports
- Where a department stands in relation to others

USA Today found that this last method alone improved performance![5]
What are some other ways you can let employees know how they are doing and make them informed and committed members of your service quality team?

- Feedback on performance goals (charts, graphs, and other visual affirmations). For example, CountryFair Theme Park displays a 50 × 10 foot graph of guest satisfaction ratings, updated daily.
- Service quality reminders. The one we like best is inside the kitchen at Marriott's Camelback Inn. It says in one-foot high letters, "If you don't like its looks, don't serve it." Some companies use preprinted posters, which you can buy from catalogues.
- Letters of appreciation from customers, posted for all to see.
- Writeups in company newsletters.
- Monthly informal get-togethers or "rap" sessions to report progress, answer questions, and otherwise keep people informed. (This is probably the best way to arrest and prevent rumors.)

• And of course, all types of formal recognition and rewards—which we discuss in Chapter 16.

In summary, information is the lifeblood of an organization. It is crucial in many of our steps: internal evaluation, determining customer requirements, establishing goals and measurements, etc. Information needs to be two-way. Feedback—to and from employees—ties it all together and integrates the organization.

Notes

1. Philip B. Crosby, *Quality Without Tears* (New York: McGraw-Hill, 1984), p. 112.
2. Tom Peters and Nancy Austin, *A Passion for Excellence* (New York: Random House, 1985).
3. Kenneth Blanchard and Spencer Johnson, *The One Minute Manager* (New York: William Morrow, 1982).
4. Philip G. Hanson, "Giving Feedback: An Interpersonal Skill" in John E. Jones and J. William Pfeiffer, eds., *The 1975 Annual Handbook for Group Facilitators* (San Diego: University Press, 1975), p. 147.
5. Donald B. Berryman, "A New Commitment to the Customer," in Jay Sprechler, *When American Does It Right* (Norcross, Ga.: Industrial Engineering and Management Press, 1988), p. 442.

Sixteen

Step 11: Recognition, Rewards, Celebrations

Once you're achieving results, it's time for recognition, rewards, and cel-ebrations—the eleventh step in the master strategy.

In this chapter, we describe some general guidelines for this process, discuss specific examples, and then detail a New Attitude Day.

Guidelines for Rewards

Open to Everyone

Everyone likes prizes. If you visit the office of an expert sailor, sales-person, or bridge player, chances are you'll see trophies prominently dis-played. Prizes are great motivators—and not just big rewards for big performances. Modest rewards are invaluable for recognizing those people and groups who meet the goals and for everyone who is doing a good job.

For what do you give rewards? In addition to rewarding obvious achievements like meeting thirty-day, sixty-day, and ninety-day goals, on-the-job improvement, and high levels of productivity, try to come up with creative ways to reward. Also change both *what* you reward and the re-wards themselves at least every six months.

There are many creative ways to reward. Here are some examples:

1. Establish a goal for how many days a department can go without an order-entry error. Post the number of error-free days on a scoreboard so their colleagues can see it and congratulate them.
2. Start an "on-time club." Enroll any group that is on time for an entire week.

While you want to recognize all kinds of achievement, you especially want to notice extraordinary achievement. How can you do this?

Some organizations have different levels of rewards. For example, everyone who participates in a program gets a lapel pin. Those in the top 40 percent get a plaque, and those in the top 5 percent a ring.

Sometimes this leads to more than 5 percent getting the top award, so the company creates new awards. If you have bronze, silver, and gold clubs, and everyone seems to be making them, wonderful! Don't stiffen the requirements; create double bronze, double silver, and double gold clubs, or special bronze, silver, and gold circle awards.

Be careful you are rewarding behavior that matches organizational goals. One supermarket told its cashiers to give each customer individual attention but rewarded them for the number of items processed per hour. So cashiers rushed customers through instead of helping them. It also "inspired" them to find ways to beat the system, i.e., punching in each can in a six-pack to increase their output per hour.

Use Ceremony

If you just call someone into your office and hand over a certificate, it's nice, but . . . People love—and want—ceremony. Here's how some companies do it.

IBM produces films on its top ten salespeople, including their hobbies and families. It shows them at a banquet for its other top people. IBM also has a President's Club for its top salespeople and keeps score so that 75 percent of its salespeople are members.[1]

Waste Management, Inc.'s annual report features watercolor portraits of employees who deserve special recognition. This includes those who serve noncustomers, like a truck driver who saved someone's life.[2]

The Limited Stores has an annual celebration for its top 100 store managers (out of about 600). They are invited to the annual President's Club meeting, a gala that takes place each August in Vail, Colorado. The highlight of the meeting is the presentation of awards to the top managers. They are brought by a ski lift to the top of a mountain, where the awards ceremony takes place, with video cameras recording every second of it. A memorable occasion, to put it mildly. And the film is used to spur on the whole system.[3]

The ceremony doesn't have to be a formal occasion:[4]

- One manager replaced all his staff's chairs one by one: As staff members increased their output, they were summoned to the boss's office, told to sit in their new chair, and then rolled back to their work station by the boss.
- An executive recruiting firm bought beautiful old French taxicab horns. Whenever a staff member fills a job, the boss blows the horn ceremoniously.

The "ceremony" doesn't have to be a public hoopla. Anything that lets people know that others recognize their achievement will do.

Paul Revere (Insurance) Companies has a program called PEET: Program for Ensuring that Everyone's Thanked. Each Monday morning, it issues a PEET Sheet showing what each team is doing. Every member of the executive committee, including the president, makes it a point to visit three team leaders and discuss their accomplishments each week.[5]

Domino's Pizza, Inc. holds a Distribution Olympics to crown champion pizza-makers. Employees compete in fourteen areas, including Veggie Slicing, Traffic Management, Dough Making and Catching, Accounting, and Interpersonal Skills. Winners get $4000 each or a vacation for two. The parent company now has over 3,000 franchisees, and the distribution subsidiary has a 95 percent share of the market.[6]

And the celebration doesn't even have to be tied to achievement all the time. Anything that lets employees know you appreciate them tends to boost morale.

The head of a fifteen-person accounting department reports excellent results from holding a celebration at least once a week. It may be for a work achievement, or it may be somebody's birthday. Even something as modest as a box of donuts does the trick.

Be Sincere

If the award means something to you, it will mean something to the recipient.

One manager loves books. He rewards achievements with personally selected first editions. Even colleagues who don't like to read appreciate this personal touch.[7]

Jay Johnson of Crest Microfilm (Cedar Rapids, Iowa) combines feedback and rewards. Every month he hosts a get-together. If it's been an okay month, he orders pizza and soft drinks. But if the company has done very well, he lets employees choose the menu.[8]

Merit awards have to be earned. Ask an employee of the month why he or she got that award. If they say, "It was my turn," you know your awards are not serving their intended function.

That's why some organizations have colleagues or customers choose the winners. They are often a lot closer to what's going on than management.

Money Is Not Always the Best Reward

If you want to give money, it's best to give it to everyone on a team. Giving individuals cash awards leads to win-lose competitive behavior: People stop cooperating with colleagues in an effort to outdo them. All the workers who help an individual winner resent the fact that they contributed and got nothing. On the other hand, people will work hard for months to earn a T-shirt if it means something.

Computervision (now part of Prime Computer, Inc.) gave clear plastic pens filled with ground-up dollar bills as performance prizes at regular monthly meetings. People who won one wouldn't even let colleagues borrow it—they could only look at it.

One of the most creative ideas for a reward is used by manager Wynn Tyner at Marriott's Camelback Inn. Each day, one guest (selected randomly) is given the "Gold Key" and invited to reward any employee who that guest feels has provided outstanding service. All employees— waiters, maids, gardeners, hairdressers, bellboys, valet parkers, cooks— are eligible and, of course, all of them know it. And that key is always circulating. When it is awarded by a guest, the employee returns it to the manager's office for a cash prize. All recipients are honored at the monthly employee meeting.

Rewarding Your Producers

Here are some spectacular examples of how some companies have chosen to reward staff:[9]

After its big turnaround, SAS held parties in three countries for all its 16,000 employees. It gave each of them a gold watch and sent them home in a private limousine.

When Oxford Software of New Jersey passed the $10 million mark, it took all 125 employees to Acapulco, Mexico, to celebrate.

Marriott Hotels finds that shares of company stock are motivating. Everyone in the company will try to do a better job if they know their performance will influence the price of their stock.[10]

Nordstrom's, legendary for service, each month honors exceptional salespeople, who get $100 and substantial discounts in Nordstrom's upscale stores. Nordstrom's has a hall of fame for great service, called a Pace Setter Club, and encourages workers to praise each other's efforts in memos called "Heroics." Stores judged best by customers' letters, thankyou notes, and peer ratings are given cash rewards.

One West Coast company (Koda Productions) specializes in making home movies of outstanding service providers. It secretly interviews the star's family, colleagues, and old friends for a "This Is Your Career" movie.[11]

Finally, there's the Southland Corporation. Its "secret shoppers" visited all their 7-Eleven stores. If they received good treatment, they gave the contact person a prize on the spot and entered the store in a drawing from which one store from each of their regions was picked.

The seventeen winners went to Dallas for the finals. There they participated in a game show, hosted by Monty Hall of TV's "Let's Make a Deal." Just as on the TV show, each got to choose a "door" that concealed a prize, and then one name was drawn for the grand prize—$1 million. The entire ceremony was videotaped and shown on TV news around the country.[12]

New Attitude Day

New Attitude Day (NAD) is a public celebration of your commitment to your customers.

The primary purpose of New Attitude Day is to demonstrate your commitment to your customers and to announce goals, rewards, and celebrations. A second purpose is to motivate employees to commit themselves to service quality excellence. So the day really celebrates a turning point.

When the organization has made sufficient progress on the master strategy steps to show there's something new in the air, the network members schedule New Attitude Day. In addition to all employees, they invite employees' families, union officials, politicians, important customers, and suppliers. They publicize the coming event on local TV, radio, and press, and invite media coverage. They make sure supervisors and managers are sufficiently informed about the day that they can answer employee questions. And finally, they might whip up interest (perhaps through a poster or slogan contest).

In large corporations, each division can have its own New Attitude Day. The best way to schedule NAD is to close down and hold it during normal working hours. This really demonstrates your commitment. And dress your place up, so everyone knows something special is happening.

A typical New Attitude Day:

1. *Top management welcome.* Remember, the purpose of the day is to demonstrate top management commitment to customer-drivenness. It starts with the chief executive officer of the organization, who makes a brief speech, perhaps five minutes, to kick off the event. The speech mentions goals, rewards for those who help achieve them, and the celebrations planned when goals are met. If you are holding the event at numerous locations, the speech can be on videotape.

2. *Guest speakers.* We suggest you invite union officials, politicians, customers, and suppliers, as well as employees' families. Ask one or two well-known guests to speak, to congratulate you and say how pleased they are that your organization is renewing its commitment to customers. Again keep it brief—less than five minutes.

3. *Individual commitments.* Once management has demonstrated its commitment and enthusiasm, invite each individual employee to participate as a charter partner in your new customer-driven service program. (Note that this is only an invitation; don't pressure your employees. This is *not* a union election, community chest drive, or religious revival.) As charter partners, they'll receive a memento, such as a cap, T-shirt, lapel pin, or plaque, and have their named entered on the permanent charter partner register displayed in your main lobby or cafeteria. You might also get a large banner or plaque and invite any who want to sign it. Later you'll post it where all can see.

4. *Fun and games.* This can include a picnic, awards, skits or a TV-style game show on service, a band (perhaps a member can write an NAD song), a parade, a boatride or hayride, fireworks, or a skywriter or airplane carrying a banner saying, "Happy New Attitude Day."

Finally, you might videotape the festivities. You're going to be holding celebrations on the anniversary of New Attitude Day, and you can show the video of the original NAD then.

Motivation

The question sometimes arises: "Why all the hoopla? Does it take all this to motivate people?"

To answer this, let's look briefly at motivation and resistance to change.

What do you think motivates your people? Turn to Worksheet 36 and list the motivating factors in question 1.

Another question: What excites you about your work? What motivates you? List your responses in question 2.

Did "money" appear, at least on the employee list? Money can sometimes motivate, but money isn't the only or chief motivator. There are many things people won't do for money, like hurt a friend, abandon their loved ones, or jump ten feet off the ground. Throughout history, money has not been an effective long-term motivator.[13]

Lists 1 and 2 in Worksheet 36 are probably different. Obviously, you put a lot more effort into your job than what your job description requires. Chances are you work for your personal satisfaction, a feeling of accomplishment, recognition, and financial security.

Now if these are the factors that motivate you to work, what do you think makes your people less motivated than you?

Most managers say things like, "They don't feel as important"; "Their job is too routine"; "They don't see the big picture"; "They don't

Worksheet 36. What Motivates People

1. What do you think motivates your people? List the motivating factors:

_____

_____

_____

_____

_____

2. What excites you about your work? What motivates *you*?

_____

_____

_____

_____

Reprinted by courtesy of Learning Dynamics, Inc.

have contact with top executives"; "They're not as committed to the organization."

Your New Attitude Day and your continuing rewards program can be remedies for these malaises. They make people feel more important. It breaks up the routine. It shows them the big picture. It exposes them to top executives, and it brings out a commitment to the organization.

Change

The other reason for New Attitude Day is people's attitude toward change.[14] People often resist change and fear the adjustment to change that's needed.

What can you do to overcome resistance to change?

- Involve as many people as possible in the process, i.e., through your network. Participation leads to ownership and commitment.
- Communicate clearly and often the purpose of the change.
- Communicate exactly what you expect and require of your people. Avoid surprises.

Worksheet 37. Change

To identify barriers to change, check the problems below that you are most likely to have, and then in Part B match each with the solutions.

Part A: Why People Resist Change

_____ 1. *Loss of Control*
When people feel on top of things, change threatens them with losing control of their personal bailiwick.

_____ 2. *Uncertainty*
Predictability is comforting to many people. Change brings uncertainty, which some people find threatening.

_____ 3. *Surprise*
We like new things, but hate surprises. Sudden change is very unsettling to most of us.

_____ 4. *Habits*
We love our habits. They are efficient and don't require thought. Establishing new behavior patterns is difficult.

_____ 5. *Familiarity*
The more we know things, the better we like them. (That's why companies spend a lot on advertising.) The unfamiliar is disturbing.

_____ 6. *Work*
New things usually mean more work (at least at the beginning).

_____ 7. *Competence*
People know they can do what they already do. Change means they will have to master new skills, and they don't know if they will be able to do it.

_____ 8. *Ripples*
People fear that change in one thing will lead to changes in others. (And they're right; that's the dynamic system.)

_____ 9. *Adjustment*
People are afraid it will take them a long time to adjust to any change.

Part B: Overcoming Resistance to Change

Place the numbers that you checked in Part A next to the strategies that will best fit them.

_____ Participation leads to ownership and commitment. Involve as many people as you can in the process.

_____ Communicate—clearly and often—the purpose of the change.

_____ Communicate exactly what you expect of people. Avoid surprises.

_____ Divide major change into manageable steps. (Make sure the first steps succeed.)

_____ Don't try to force people to pledge allegiance at the beginning. Let commitment grow.

_____ Be a model. Demonstrate your commitment to the change, and show your willingness to change yourself.

_____ Reward progress. Reinforce efforts to do things the new way.

_____ Find role models. Look for people who have already changed. Publicly commend them and let them guide others.

_____ Commit resources. Change takes time, energy, and support. Make them available.

_____ Honor the past. Don't badmouth old ways of doing things. Allow for nostalgia, even grief. Then build excitement for the future.

Reprinted by courtesy of Learning Dynamics, Inc.

- Divide any major change into manageable steps. (Make sure the first steps succeed.)
- Encourage, but don't force, people to pledge allegiance at the beginning. Let commitment grow.
- Be a model. Demonstrate your commitment to the change, and show your willingness to change yourself.
- Reward progress. Reinforce efforts to do things the new way.
- Find as many role models as possible. Look for people who have already changed. Publicly commend them and let them guide others.
- Commit resources. Change takes time, money, energy, and management support. Make them available.
- Honor the past. Allow for nostalgia and the good old days. Then build excitement for the future.

Look now at Worksheet 37, "Change." Check the problems in Part A you are most likely to have, and then match each with the solutions in Part B.

At this point, your strategy for keeping customers for life is almost complete. You've made all the changes to improve service quality and celebrated your success with rewards and celebrations for those who were responsible. All that remains now is to institutionalize this new attitude and new way of doing things. In Step 12, we describe a network that supports continuous improvement.

Notes

1. Tom Peters and Nancy Austin, *A Passion for Excellence* (New York: Random House, 1985), p. 255.
2. "Employee Relations," *Customers!*, September 1987, p. 5.
3. Peters and Austin, *A Passion for Excellence*, p. 253.

4. *Ibid.*, p. 258.
5. *Ibid,* p. 256.
6. Tom Peters, *Skunks in Action* (Palo Alto, Calif.: TPG Communications, 1986), p. 6.
7. Peters and Austin, *A Passion for Excellence,* p. 260.
8. "Managing People," *Inc.*, October 1987, p. 142.
9. Peters and Austin, *A Passion for Excellence,* Chapter 15.
10. G. M. Hostage, "Quality Control in a Service Business," *Harvard Business Review,* July–August 1975.
11. Mike Bowker, "Golden Carrots: What's Up in Incentive Programs," *Human Resource Executive,* September 1989.
12. "Thanks a Million," public relations package from 7-Eleven, February 1987.
13. Christopher Hegarty, *How to Manage Your Boss* (New York: Ballantine, 1985), p. 96.
14. Ron Zemke, *Service Excellence Workbook* (Waltham, Mass.: Performance Research Associates, 1986), pp. 39–41.

Seventeen

Step 12: A Continuous Improvement Network

Today's manager often needs to work with different departments, levels, and functions. This means you have another new role to play in addition to Customer-Champion and Coach-Counselor—Integrator. We use "integrator," rather than "coordinator," because you have to do more than "coordinate" conflicting entities. To integrate the process and to assure continuous improvement, you have to meld cross-functional groups together. This is the twelfth and final step in the master strategy.

We hear about project and matrix management, but the integration involves more. Project management brings people from different functional departments together temporarily. Matrix management is difficult to define, but basically:

> Each matrix [manager] is in charge of an entire function, product, area, or service, but is not in total command over the individuals who report to him or her. The matrix boss shares power with an equal, often over the same subordinates and usually over information and issues.[1]

In the customer-driven organization, employees' first loyalty is to customers, not to an organizational chart. On paper they may report to a regional manager, who reports to a vice-president, who reports to the president. But everyone knows that the real boss is the customer, so they're more interested in getting things done than in organizational protocol. They cross boundary lines and work together to do whatever it takes to delight customers.

Most organizational conflicts occur between peers because there are no rules to govern peer relationships as there are with bosses and subordinates. Here are some guidelines for reducing conflict and "managing horizontally":

1. *Treat other departments as customers and suppliers.* We've been emphasizing the internal customer-supplier relationship. But suppose the other department were your only customer? How would you treat them if they were the ultimate user? How would you treat them if they were an outside supplier?

2. *Learn from mistakes.* If you disappoint another department, find out how you can improve your performance. Share information with colleagues, listen to them, and treat them with respect, without being defensive.

3. *Train others to meet your needs.* If other departments let you down, let them know about it constructively. Tell them exactly what you need from them. Instead of using their failure as an excuse or instead of pinpointing blame, help them. A customer-driven organization helps customers operate more efficiently. A customer-driven manager shows others in the organization how they can work better with each other.

Managing a Cross-Functional Network

Being an integrator requires a new set of skills. To understand what they are, let's look first at what a "team" is and then at what its manager does.

The team concept, of course, comes from sports, and it's an instructive term. Every sports season, a diverse group of individuals reports to training camp. The coach's job is to mold these individuals into a team. To do it, coaches:

- Communicate a common purpose
- Assign roles based on talents
- Get the team to integrate its skills to accentuate individual strengths and minimize weaknesses
- Use immediate feedback (scores) to correct problems (that is, realize you have to do something different if you're losing)
- Build synergy; problem-solve together
- Create a nonjudgmental atmosphere
- Minimize territoriality and blaming
- Build a common language and purpose
- Set milestones and deadlines

This is exactly how an integrating manager forms a successful network.

We like the idea of a network better than team because teams usually compete. A network, on the other hand, comprises people working to-

Figure 17-1.   What managers do.

Traditional	*Network*
Focuses on current goals.	Focuses on vision.
Is reactive.	Is proactive.
Limits participation by others.	Promotes involvement.
Resents "know-it-alls."	Seeks excellence.
Solves problems.	Facilitates.
Controls information.	Communicates.
Ignores conflict.	Mediates conflict.
May recognize achievements.	Quickly recognizes achievements.
Advises group only.	Keeps commitments.

Reprinted by courtesy of Learning Dynamics, Inc.

gether to achieve a common goal, committed to helping each other with whatever resources they have available.

You need people to integrate and continuously improve the service quality improvement process. No one person can do it alone. But a network of committed people can provide motivation, implementation, and the clout to keep the process moving. Working as a network serves customers best because it can:

- Prevent duplication of effort
- Avoid conflicts between divisions
- Reduce false starts
- Allow people to convey information only once

Figure 17-1 highlights the differences between the roles of a traditional department manager and a network leader.

Traditional managers are totally focused on current goals. Network leaders, on the other hand, keep their eye on the company's mission as well as short-term goals.

Traditional managers react to upper management, peers, and subordinates. Network leaders anticipate needs and inspire others to go beyond individual concerns.

Traditional managers limit the size of roles others can play in planning. Network leaders get others involved—and committed.

Traditional managers may resent or distrust employees who know more than they do. Network leaders look for top people and encourage them to excel.

Traditional managers think problem solving is their prerogative. Network leaders empower subordinates to solve problems, because they know subordinates have better information, being closer to the customer.

Traditional managers control information and communicate only what they think subordinates need to know. Network leaders communicate openly.

Traditional managers ignore or suppress conflict. Network leaders deal with conflict (both intra- and inter-group) before it becomes destructive.

Traditional managers recognize accomplishments slowly, if at all. Network leaders go out of their way to recognize individual and group achievements.

And traditional managers change group agreements, if it's convenient for them. Network leaders honor their commitments—and expect others to do so.

Selling the Service Imperative

To initiate customer-driven culture company-wide, you will need other managers on your side.

You literally need their "buy-in," because they will probably have to pay for the costs of quality service out of their budget. So service quality lives and dies by management support. If you don't have it, you need to "sell" the deal.

To increase management buy-in, you need to:[2]

1. *Assess your internal customers' needs.* Everyone has internal customers, including managers. Learn what your internal customers require of you and your subordinates and make sure you supply it.

2. *Know your organization's mission and objectives.* (You can use this as a powerful argument to gain support.)

3. *Develop a departmental mission statement and a presentation.* Develop facts, figures, and a short presentation on customer-driven service, based on your area of responsibility.

4. *Show other managers how customer-driven service benefits them.* Don't talk features, talk benefits: What's in it for them? (Some possible benefits are listed in Figure 17-2).

5. *Point out the costs of poor service.* You are the expert, so let people know the costs and benefits of your efforts to improve service.

6. *Be proactive by sharing information.* Don't wait for people to come to you.

Figure 17-2. Benefits of customer-driven service excellence.

Providing customer-driven service:

- Makes you more important to the organization
- Promotes career and earnings
- Reduces stress
- Teaches important skills
- Makes your job easier
- Enables you to influence others
-

Keeps your customers for life

Reprinted by courtesy of Learning Dynamics, Inc.

One good way is to share the customer information you gather. This often will point up service needs. Take the initiative to help other managers meet those needs; don't wait for them to come to you.

7. *Share both responsibility and credit.* Involve other managers in improving service quality from the start. And when your strategy succeeds, publicize both the results achieved and who helped make it happen.

8. *Be a role model yourself for the skills you're teaching.* Treat your internal customers very, very well.

9. *Focus on what the organization and customers need, rather than what you need.* Your job is to serve customers. "Service" is not an end in itself.

10. *Publicize your efforts internally.* Use bulletin boards, newsletters, and the grapevine to let everyone know what great results your efforts are producing.

11. *Present certificates of achievement for completed training and problem-solving programs.* These really mean something to most people. They'll display them—and remember where they got them.

12. *Evaluate your programs, and share the results.* This helps you prove the value of service excellence, as well as weed out less successful activities.

Enlisting Support

A number of techniques are useful in getting bosses and peers—anyone you don't manage—to support you:

1. *Onion patch.* If you're the only one standing up for customers, you may feel like a "lonely petunia in an onion patch." If so, the remedy is to "think big, but stick close to your roots."

Work on customer-focused projects that are within your span of control, that are also effective enough to capture senior management's attention, i.e., projects with big dollar implications. Involve others in your efforts and share the credit with them. Build a network of believers and supporters while you make real improvements in the system. Stay alert to any requests from higher-ups to explain what you're doing. Have articles, pictures, and tapes on hand. Prepare a presentation that you can adapt from fifteen to ninety minutes. It's even better if you can get enthusiastic subordinates to run the presentation. Identify the most likely objections and questions and have answers ready. The object of onion patch is to make believers and Customers-Champions out of top management. Without their support, "all of your transformation efforts will wither on the vine."[3]

2. *Snowballing.* For projects outside your immediate area, you'll need the support of others, perhaps someone in a higher position or in another department. To enlist support, sell one manager on the idea, then show other managers how much their colleagues are chipping in. This builds up a bandwagon effect that managers don't want to miss. Ask others for conditional support: They may agree, for example, to pledge budget or staff if higher management approves a rollout.

As the effort becomes successful, show the results to top managers. Although top people don't have to sponsor you, you need their support to get very far. This support may be tacit; for instance, they may simply show up at your meetings. It may be conditional, like a boss saying, "If you can get others to go along, it's okay with me." Or it may be active, like the boss selling others on the idea (sometimes rehearsed by you).

3. *Tin cupping.* With this strategy, you act as though you're not sure what to do. (It's also called the "Columbo approach," because in the TV detective show, Columbo is always saying things like, "I must be stupid, but I don't understand . . ." Answers that suspects give to Columbo's "dumb" questions reveal their secrets.) Go to department managers and ask them to help you figure out how to be more customer-focused. By involving them at the planning stage, you gain their buy-in to the plan because it seems more their idea. Keep these "owners" of the project apprised through progress reports. Also realize that you are indebted to them—if only for giving you their advice—and return the favor when needed.

Figure 17-3 summarizes these techniques.
What are you going to do next? The following three "Personal Action" worksheets (38, 39, and 40) will help you get started in your new integrator role and on putting customer-driven service into place.

Figure 17-3. Enlisting support.

Onion patch technique

1. Select efforts that are within your span of control but that are effective enough to capture the attention of higher managers.
2. Involve others in your efforts.
3. Share the credit with them.
4. Build a network while you make real improvements.
5. Stay alert to any requests from higher-ups to explain what you're doing.
6. Identify the most likely objections and questions, and have answers ready.

Snowballing

1. Sell one manager on the idea.
2. Show other managers how much their colleagues are chipping in.
3. Ask others to pledge budget or staff if higher management approves a rollout.
4. Show successful results to top managers.

Tin cupping ("Columbo")

1. Answer "What's in it for me?"
2. Make everyone an owner.
3. Provide feedback on progress.
4. Return the favor.

Reprinted by courtesy of Learning Dynamics, Inc.

Establishing a Network in a Large Company

The network integrates the customer-driven service improvement process by coordinating efforts, removing stumbling blocks, and resolving cross-functional disputes.

Therefore, enlist members who are sold on the customer-driven strategy and who have enough clout to remove obstacles. You'll need people who can get things done, either through their position power, political savvy, or union strength.

The network sets the overall goals, objectives, and strategies of the process. It also represents the company to the outside world—the community (through special events), the media, employees' families, and others—to show the company's commitment to service and quality. In addition, it decides who needs what training, decides motivation strategies, creates company-wide celebration events, and delivers rewards.

To establish a network, you need to:

1. *Enlist members.* Let it be known that membership in the network is a plum assignment. It really is a reward for top performers, since the

Worksheet 38. Personal Action: Integrator

List five areas where you need to act as integrator. Below each, plan how you will improve relations with customers, both internal and external.

1. _____

   _____

2. _____

   _____

3. _____

   _____

4. _____

   _____

5. _____

   _____

Reprinted by courtesy of Learning Dynamics, Inc.

future of the organization lies in service quality. In some cases, the manager of each department might be a good choice, but you don't want just managers. Every department and function needs representation, so mix it up: a contact person, a secretary, and a truck driver. (Membership in the network changes, so other people will get a chance to serve too.)

2. *Educate the members in the customer-driven management 12-Step Strategy.* Network members need training. Each member represents his or her department. And they bring departmental concerns back to the network. Each member can also "adopt" one of the twelve strategy steps in detail and oversee it as it comes up. Most important, network members serve as role models for the rest of the organization in delivering customer-driven service and quality.

3. *Hire or appoint an administrator.* The network needs an administrator to set the agenda and to communicate with senior managers. In addition, the administrator schedules meetings, coordinates efforts between departments, and is responsible for feedback, communication, and distribution of information, such as agendas and results. In very large companies, this can best be handled by a full-time person hired for the job. In smaller companies, someone can handle it part-time, with some help. And even if you don't have a network, you need someone to be the chief customer officer (about which more a little further on).

Worksheet 39. Personal Action: Next Steps

Instructions:

Identify five positive steps you can take, beginning tomorrow, to start making your organization more customer-driven. Make sure that you check the focus of each step, and that you have at least one step directed toward external customers.

1. _____

   _____

   _____

   Focus: Internal   External   Employees   Peers
             Customers   Customers

2. _____

   _____

   _____

   Focus: Internal   External   Employees   Peers
             Customers   Customers

3. _____

   _____

   _____

   Focus: Internal   External   Employees   Peers
             Customers   Customers

4. _____

   _____

   _____

(continues)

Worksheet 39 (*continued*)

☐	☐	☐	☐

Focus: Internal   External   Employees   Peers
             Customers   Customers

5. _____

_____

_____

☐	☐	☐	☐

Focus: Internal   External   Employees   Peers
             Customers   Customers

Reprinted by courtesy of Learning Dynamics, Inc.

4. *Agree on a charter and job descriptions.* Network members agree on its purpose, membership, relationships, responsibilities, and meetings. (Figure 17-4 shows a sample charter.) However, they do *not* serve as dictators or police watchdogs, nor do they pre-approve every move. They are there to be resources to other managers.

5. *Integrate the 12-Step Strategy.* The network members develop a plan for implementing each step and present it to the CEO or designated leader for acceptance and support.

6. *Continue to meet regularly and monitor progress.* Here are some tips on effective network meetings:

- Leave titles outside the door. Everyone is a valuable member. Do not speak in order of seniority.
- Keep remarks relevant to the topic under discussion. If people start to get off track, ask, "What is the purpose of the meeting?"
- Have an agenda and stick to the schedule.
- Keep minutes and circulate them.
- Do not get stuck in problem solving. Let each department solve problems.
- Do not make this a staff meeting.
- Make decisions by consensus; try to get all members committed to decisions under discussion.
- Take turns speaking; avoid side conversations.
- Encourage different viewpoints.

Worksheet 40. Personal Action: Worst Case Analysis

Instructions:

1. Brainstorm all the ways you can think of to keep your improvement plan from working. This includes any possible ways that others may scuttle it. For the moment, the ideas can be as outlandish as you can imagine.
2. Now go back and identify the three most likely ways that this plan may be undone.
3. Develop a plan for preventing each one of these occurrences.

Disaster I: _____

_____

Prevention plan: _____

_____

Disaster II: _____

_____

Prevention plan: _____

_____

Disaster III: _____

_____

Prevention plan: _____

_____

Figure 17-4.   Sample network charter.

Purpose

To promote, supervise, and coordinate the master strategy for keeping customers for life.

Membership

Department managers will name a representative from each department. Members will select the chairperson, who will name an administrator.

All members will have taken the Service Excellence course. They will serve for one year.

Responsibilities

1. Establish a charter.
2. Write job descriptions.
3. Promote and coordinate service quality training.
4. Promote commitment to keeping customers for life.
5. Ensure that plans are consistent with the organization's mission.
6. Make recommendations on resources needed to implement plans.
7. Coordinate implementation within each department.
8. Monitor problems and successes and make recommendations.
9. Plan for continuity with the next network.

Meetings

The network will meet at least once a week to review plans and progress.

The administrator will circulate an agenda before each meeting. Meetings will stick to the agenda.

The administrator will take minutes and circulate them to all members of the network.

Reprinted by courtesy of Learning Dynamics, Inc.

The network chooses the most appropriate measures on which to concentrate—usually customer feedback and the cost of poor service. This lets the network members know how well the process is doing.

The Structure of Networks

The structure of your network will reflect your organization. Here are two examples from leaders in the service improvement process.

IBM Canada

IBM Canada employs about 12,000 people, three-fourths of them in nonmanufacturing areas. Their service improvement system is shown in Figure 17-5.[4]

Figure 17-5.   IBM Canada.

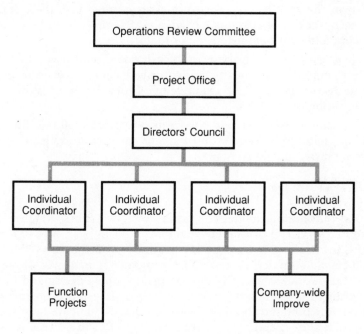

Reprinted by courtesy of Learning Dynamics, Inc.

At the top is an Operations Review Committee, which we would call the Customer for Life Council. It's an executive-level committee, headed by the CEO and those who report directly to him or her. The committee sets guidelines for the service quality process, reviews progress, and makes policy decisions.

A project office supports the council and oversees the entire service improvement process.

The next level is the Directors' Council, nominated by the individual group leaders. It crosses functional boundaries outside the normal management system, resolving disputes and ensuring consistent implementation. The Directors' Council deals with major issues and changes in policies, strategies, and systems.

This is also the group that talks to the outside world, communicating about the improvement process. The Directors' Council will form task forces to deal with special problems.

IBM notes that problems may be departmental, functional, or companywide. So it has three levels of quality efforts:

1. *Individual coordinators,* representing major functional areas of IBM, form the core of the process. Managers meet with their departments each week to discuss quality activities. Examples include reducing paperwork and coordinating customer inquiries.

2. *Function projects* are those problems that extend beyond one department's boundaries. They typically involve major processes or procedures across the company. An example of a function project is reviewing credit-granting procedures.

3. *Companywide improvement projects* involve more than one function. Improving billing procedures and making equipment available to customers are cross-functional efforts.

Florida Power & Light

A second outstanding model is Florida Power & Light's.[5] (Figure 17-6 shows FPL's service improvement system.)

FPL is a leading nuclear power producer with thirteen plants and 113 offices and service centers. The company is naturally organized around teamwork within and among work groups. FPL wanted to preserve existing reporting systems, so it formed quality improvement teams based on function and location. Thus the quality improvement framework parallels the corporate structure. Each of FPL's five divisions covers a separate part of the state, and each division has a number of districts.

At the top of this structure is a Quality Council consisting of senior managers, at least one from each division. The Quality Council sets policy and is the final arbiter on quality issues.

Each division (or department) has a Leaders' Group, chaired by its manager. Managers of each function staff these groups. In FPL's case, this includes transmission/distribution, engineering, and customer service. The Leaders' Groups address their own problems, as well as problems referred to them by lower-level groups.

FPL also has Corporate Issue Groups, in which managers address issues affecting the entire company. Leaders' Group members suggest issues these groups should deal with (and then often volunteer to serve on the team). Corporate Issues Groups use the same process as the Leaders' Groups. They recommend changes in corporate systems and policies, such as customer requirements, goals, and employee relations.

There are three kinds of lower groups:

1. *Functional* groups take responsibility for identifying and solving problems in their individual work locations.
2. *Cross-Functional* groups do the same thing on a broader basis.
3. *Task* groups are formed on an ad hoc basis to solve specific problems.

Figure 17-6.   Florida Power & Light.

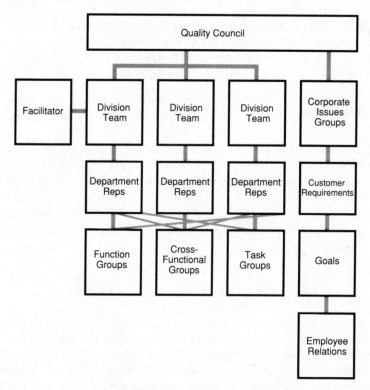

Reprinted by courtesy of Learning Dynamics, Inc.

All teams meet regularly under an elected team leader. A program facilitator—an in-house expert on quality improvement techniques— helps them organize programs and establish links with other groups. They determine when to call in people from other work functions and when to pass problems on to a higher level.

These are just two possible models. Your own network needs to fit your organizational size and framework.

Other Structures

Two years ago, Learning Dynamics held extensive interviews with about 200 corporations reputed to be quality leaders in their industry.

Our interviewers found that virtually all of these companies have a formal quality improvement process in place. (However, most of these companies did not incorporate customer information into their quality improvement process.*)

Although most companies in their industries centralize market research, the best organizations have *de*centralized this function.†

As for the quality improvement structure itself, three basic models emerged, each covering about a third of the companies.

1. *Centralized model.* In these organizations, policies and goals are handed down from the top, though it is the job of each unit to implement them.

2. *Decentralized model.* These companies make each operating unit responsible for quality improvement. Typically, units organized by forming ongoing improvement teams which, in turn, form task teams for specific problems.

3. *Decentralized with coordination model.* Here the unit is the heart of the process, but there are companywide committees of quality improvement coordinators.

Who Will Be the Chief Customer Officer?

As a manager, you have the power to get things done within your department and your organization. Who better than the customer to get things done for? You may be high up in your organization. You may have a six-figure salary and an industrywide reputation. Still it's the customer who signs your paycheck. So, every manager needs to push for what's best for the customer, because without customers, the organization will cease to exist. The final three Personal Action worksheets (41, 42, and 43) will help. But to maintain your company's competitive advantage in today's tough new economic environment, somebody needs to represent the customer within the organization—to be the Chief Customer Officer (CCO). Let it be you.

---

* Exceptions include 3M, American Airlines, Disney, and Xerox.
† This includes Xerox, 3M, and Hewlett Packard.

Worksheet 41. Personal Action: What's in It for You?

Take one of your challenges from Worksheet 3 and look at the implications for yourself and your customers of solving—or not solving—the problem.

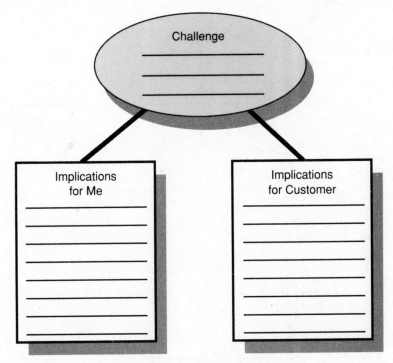

Reprinted by courtesy of Learning Dynamics, Inc.

Worksheet 42. Personal Action:
Strengths and Weaknesses

Instructions:

Fill out the strengths and weaknesses of your organization *as it currently exists* with respect to the customer.

Strengths:

_____

_____

_____

_____

_____

_____

Weaknesses:

_____

_____

_____

_____

_____

_____

_____

Worksheet 43. Personal Action: Action Planning

List all the major steps necessary to accomplish the task of driving your organization for your customers.

	Step	People	Resources Required	Mile-stones/ Dates	Success Criteria
1.					
2.					
3.					
4.					
5.					
6.					
7.					
8.					
9.					
10.					
11.					
12.					

Reprinted by courtesy of Learning Dynamics, Inc.

Notes

1. J. William Pfeiffer, ed., *A Handbook of Structured Experiences for Human Relations Training*, Volume IX (San Diego: University Associates, 1983), p. 360.
2. Halsey W. Snow, "Increasing Management Buy-In to Training," *NETWorking*, Fall 1988.
3. Peter R. Scholtes and Heero Hacquebord, "Beginning the Quality Transformation, Part I," *Quality Progress*, July 1988.
4. Sally R. Luce, "Building Quality Through People," Conference Board of Canada, September 1985, Part 3.
5. "Florida Power & Light Company," American Productivity Center Case Study 39, 1984.

Appendix:

Survey Summary

In 1988, Learning Dynamics, Inc., conducted a "Customer Commitment Survey." A total of 180 managers from eighty-six companies responded.

Survey participants agreed that the quality of service in the United States was not very good (75 percent rated it only fair or poor). Looking at the survey, we can see why.

- Only 57 percent rate "meeting customer needs" as their Number One priority.
- In 62 percent of the companies, not everyone is aware of what customers do with the company's product or service.
- Fewer than half of new products and services are developed or improved based on customer suggestions and complaints, despite an MIT study showing that the best innovations come from customers.
- Only 59 percent of the respondents contact lost customers; 7 percent do nothing when they lose a customer.
- In some companies (17 percent), not even salespeople talk to customers. It gets worse for senior management (22 percent don't talk to them), marketing (29 percent), and R&D (67 percent).
- Only 60 percent report they base their competitive strategy primarily on "attention to customer needs." (And they say that only 29 percent of their competitors emphasize this.) What's ironic is that 21 percent claim to base competitive strategy on product "quality," but the only way to define "quality" is to ask customers.
- Thirty-three percent say their marketing strategy "aims to produce business" from new, as opposed to repeat, customers. Now unless you're in the sterilization or funeral business, you'll be a lot better off cultivating existing customers than trying to drum up new ones (it's five times as expensive to get an order from a new customer as from an old one).

In fact, the survey serves as a manual of what companies could be doing to improve customer focus, but are not. Some examples:

- Have contact people report their observations of customer interactions (only 50 percent do).
- Use formal methods to determine customers' wants ("phone and mail

237

surveys" is the only method more than half use; 12 percent use none at all).

- Share customer research and complaints with everyone in the organization (no group does this more than eighty percent of the time now—not senior management, sales, or marketing).
- Appoint someone—preferably a chief customer officer (CCO)—to officially represent the customer's point of view within the organization. Only 10 percent have an ombudsman or CCO now; 13 percent say "no one" represents the customer.
- Have senior managers spend time with customers (only 34 percent spend more than a fourth of their time with customers now; 40 percent spend 10 percent or less).
- In determining senior managers' compensation, make "customer satisfaction" as important as goal achievement and revenue (only 3 percent put it first now; it ranks below "other").
- Use innovative ideas such as problem-solving teams, formal quality improvement programs, and individual recognition and rewards for exceptional customer service to address causes of customer dissatisfaction (less than half use any of these now).

A summary of responses to the survey follows.

Part 1: Your Organization

Percentage   *Average*
Picking as #1

1. Our highest priority for the following is (rank from 1 [highest] to 6 [lowest]):

57%	f.	Meeting customer needs	(1.8)
21%	b.	Product quality	(3.0)
18%	c.	Service quality	(2.4)
4%	a.	Cost control	(4.3)
0%	d.	Staying on schedule	(4.9)
0%	e.	Employee morale	(4.5)

2. The following people in the organization are aware of what customers do with our product or service:

38%	a.	Everyone
43%	b.	Most
19%	c.	Some
0%	d.	Few or none

3. We "listen" carefully to customers through the following informal feedback systems and act on this information (check as many as apply):

| 60% | a. | Observing them at the point of purchase/service |
| 50% | b. | Having managers spend at least one day a month visiting customers |

50% d. Having contact people report their observations
33% e. Other
6% c. Rotating personnel so that everyone waits on customers
3% f. None

4. We use the following formal research methods to determine our customers' wants, needs, and expectations (as many as apply):

69% a. Phone and mail surveys
47% d. Focus groups
35% c. Toll-free numbers
34% b. Business reply cards
27% e. Other
12% f. None

5. We use these formal research methods:

32% a. Monthly
23% d. Occasionally
22% c. About once a year
15% b. Quarterly
9% e. Never

6. The following departments receive and act on this formal and informal research (as many as apply):

79% e. Senior management
73% b. Marketing
71% a. Sales
69% g. Operations managers
35% d. Planning
33% c. Research & development
21% f. Finance
12% h. Other
5% i. None

7. The percentage of our products and services developed or improved based on customer suggestions/complaints is:

35% a. Less than 24 percent
31% b. 25–50 percent
14% c. 51–75 percent
20% d. More than 75 percent

8. When we lose a customer, we (as many as apply):

76% d. Find out why
59% c. Contact them
35% b. Usually know why
19% e. Take other action
7% a. Do nothing

9. The following department(s) talk directly to customers (as many as apply):

    83% a. Sales
    78% e. Senior management
    73% g. Operations management
    71% b. Marketing
    33% c. Research & development
    29% d. Planning
    27% h. Other
    23% f. Accounting
     0% i. None

10. We use customer complaints to drive continuous improvement, and distribute these data to the following department(s) (as many as apply):

    76% a. Sales
    76% e. Senior management
    71% g. Operations management
    66% b. Marketing
    38% c. Research & development
    34% d. Planning
    17% f. Accounting
    17% h. Other
     0% i. None

11. We base our competitive strategy on (rank from 1 [highest] to 5 [lowest]):

    60% b. Attention to customer needs   (1.6)
    21% d. Product quality   (2.3)
    12% a. Technology and innovation   (3.1)
     7% c. Price   (3.4)
     3% e. Other   (4.6)

12. Customers see us as a company known for its (rank from 1 [highest] to 5 [lowest]):

    41% b. Attention to customer needs   (1.9)
    26% d. Product quality   (2.2)
    16% a. Technology and innovation   (3.2)
    10% c. Price   (3.3)
     7% e. Other   (4.4)

13. Our marketing strategy aims to produce business as follows:

    33%   From new customers
    66%   From existing customers

14. The amount of business we get from repeat customers is:

     4% a. Under 25 percent
     9% b. 25–50 percent

27% c. 51–75 percent
60% d. Over 75 percent

15. The person in our organization who officially represents the customer's point of view is:

    41% c. Salespeople
    38% b. The customer service representatives
    24% f. Other
    13% a. No one
     3% d. An "ombudsman"
     7% e. A chief customer officer

16. The amount of time senior managers spend with customers is:

     2% a. 0
    38% b. 1–10 percent
    26% c. 11–25 percent
    26% d. 26–50 percent
     8% e. Over 50 percent

17. Senior managers' compensation depends on (rank from 1 [highest] to 5 [lowest]):

    60% c. Goal achievement   (1.6)
    29% b. Revenue   (2.0)
     6% d. Other   (3.6)
     5% a. Customer satisfaction   (2.8)

18. Our organization has the following systems or departments to ensure customer satisfaction (as many as apply):

    76% b. Customer service department
    45% d. Problem-solving teams to address causes of customer dissatisfaction
    38% e. A formal quality improvement program
    21% a. Complaint department
    31% c. Individual recognition and rewards for exceptional customer service
    11% f. Other

Part II: Your Industry

19. In our industry, customer satisfaction is more important than profit margin.

    56% a. Agree
    32% b. Disagree
    12% c. Don't know

20. The number of organizations in our industry who get feedback from customers (formal or informal) is:

41% a. Most
35% b. Some
15% c. Few
 9% d. Don't know

21. Most organizations in our industry compete on:

73% c. Price
35% d. Product quality
29% b. Attention to customer needs
21% a. Technology and innovation
 5% e. Other

Part III: The United States

22. The quality of service in this country is:

 3% a. Excellent
21% b. Good
66% c. Fair
 9% d. Poor

23. Most U.S. companies consider customer satisfaction a top priority.

38% a. Agree
62% b. Disagree

Number of companies responding: 86

Number of employees:	1–50	19%
	51–500	31%
	501–2000	24%
	2001 +	17%
What business are you in?	Manufacturing	32%
	Business services	30%

Following is a survey for you to fill out. If you wish, you may return it to the publisher, who will forward it to us. It will be included in our updated results.

Customer Commitment Survey

Thank you for participating in our survey. Remember that all answers are confidential. Please indicate the answer or answers that best fit you.

Your Organization

1. Our priority for the following is (rank from 1 [highest] to 6 [lowest])

   _____ a. cost control   _____ d. staying on schedule

   _____ b. product quality   _____ e. employee morale

   _____ c. service quality   _____ f. meeting customer needs

2. The following people in the organization are aware of what customers do with our product or service

   _____ a. everyone   _____ c. some

   _____ b. most   _____ d. few or none

3. We "listen" carefully to customers through the following *informal* feedback systems—and act on this information (check as many as apply)

   _____ a. observing them at the point of purchase/service

   _____ b. having managers spend at least one day a month visiting customers

   _____ c. rotating personnel so that everyone waits on customers

   _____ d. having contact people report their observations

   _____ e. other: _____

   _____ f. none

4. We use the following *formal* research methods to determine our customers' wants, needs, and expectations (as many as apply)

   _____ a. phone and mail surveys   _____ d. focus groups

       _____ e. other: _____

_____ b. business reply cards   _____ f. none
_____ c. toll-free numbers

5. We use these formal research methods

_____ a. monthly   _____ d. occasionally
_____ b. quarterly   _____ e. never
_____ c. about once a year

6. The following departments receive and act on this formal and informal research (as many as apply)

_____ a. sales   _____ f. finance
_____ b. marketing   _____ g. operations manage-
_____ c. research &   ment
          development   _____ h. other: _____
_____ d. planning   _____ i. none
_____ e. senior management

7. The percentage of our products and services developed or improved based on customer suggestions/complaints is

_____ a. less than 25%   _____ c. 51–75%
_____ b. 25–50%   _____ d. more than 75%

8. When we lose a customer, we (as many as apply)

_____ a. do nothing   _____ d. find out why
_____ b. usually know why   _____ e. take other action:
_____ c. contact them   _____

9. The following department(s) talk directly to customers (as many as apply)

_____ a. sales   _____ f. finance
_____ b. marketing   _____ g. operations
_____ c. research &   management
          development   _____ h. other: _____
_____ d. planning   _____ i. none
_____ e. senior management

10. We use customer complaints to drive continuous improvement, and distribute this data to the following department(s) (as many as apply)

_____ a. sales   _____ f. finance
_____ b. marketing   _____ g. operations
_____ c. research &   management
          development   _____ h. other: _____
_____ d. planning   _____ i. none
_____ e. senior management

11. We base our competitive strategy on (rank from 1 [highest] to 5 [lowest])

_____ a. technology and   _____ d. product quality
          innovation   _____ e. other: _____
_____ b. attention to customer
          needs
_____ c. price

12. Customers see us as a company known for its (rank from 1 [highest] to 5 [lowest])

_____ a. technology and   _____ d. product quality
          innovation   _____ e. other: _____
_____ b. attention to customer
          needs
_____ c. price

13. Our marketing strategy aims to produce business as follows:

_____ % from new customers   _____ % from existing
                                             customers

14. The amount of business we actually get from repeat customers is

_____ a. under 25%   _____ c. 51–75%
_____ b. 25–50%   _____ d. over 75%

15. The person in our organization who officially represents the customer's point of view is

_____ a. no one
_____ b. the customer service representative
_____ c. salespeople
_____ d. an "ombudsman"
_____ e. a chief customer officer
_____ f. other: _____

16. The amount of time senior managers spend with customers is

_____ a. 0%   _____ d. 26–50%
_____ b. 1–10%   _____ e. over 50%
_____ c. 11–25%

17. Senior managers' compensation depends on (rank from 1 [highest] to 4 [lowest])

_____ a. customer satisfaction   _____ c. goal achievement
_____ b. revenue   _____ d. other: _____

18. Our organization has the following systems or departments to ensure customer satisfaction (as many as apply)

_____ a. complaint department
_____ b. customer service department
_____ c. individual recognition and rewards for exceptional
       customer service
_____ d. problem-solving teams to address causes of customer
       dissatisfaction
_____ e. a formal quality improvement program
_____ f. other: _____

Your Industry

19. In our industry, customer satisfaction is more important than profit
    margin

    _____ a. agree   _____ b. disagree   _____ c. don't know

20. The number of organizations in our industry who get feedback
    from customers (formal or informal) is

    _____ a. most   _____ c. few
    _____ b. some   _____ d. don't know

21. Most organizations in our industry compete on

    _____ a. technology and   _____ c. price
           innovation   _____ d. product quality
    _____ b. attention to customer   _____ e. other: _____
           needs

The United States

22. The quality of service in this country is

    _____ a. excellent   _____ c. fair
    _____ b. good   _____ d. poor

23. Most U.S. companies consider customer satisfaction a top priority.

    _____ a. agree   _____ b. disagree

Name:_____

Title: _____

Organization: _____

Address: _____

_____

What business are you in? _____

Number of employees: _____

Number of customers: _____

Thank you for your participation.
Please return to:

Publisher
AMACOM Books
135 West 50th Street, 15th floor
New York, New York 10020

Index